Greater Yellowstone

N A T I O N A L   F O R E S T S

Todd Wilkinson

National Forests
— of —
America

ACKNOWLEDGMENTS

Special thanks are in order to public information officers and resource specialists on all of the seven national forests, particularly to Jack Troyer and Betty Schmidt of the Greater Yellowstone Coordinating Committee and Fred Kingwill on the Bridger-Teton National Forest. They were generous with their time and steered me to people who could help on this project.

A final note of appreciation to the staff of the Greater Yellowstone Coalition based in Bozeman. The coalition — a gutsy, non-profit organization — and the federally comprised Greater Yellowstone Coordinating Committee are making sure the ecosystem is a magical place to live and visit.

ABOUT THE AUTHOR

Todd Wilkinson is a freelance journalist based in Bozeman, Montana, who frequently writes about environmental and natural resource issues in the Northern Rockies. He is the Northern Rockies correspondent for the *Denver Post* and has written for several national magazines.

DEDICATION

To my parents and Jeanne, Irene, Mabel, and Steve, for having more of an influence than you will ever know

NATIONAL FORESTS OF AMERICA SERIES

Copyright ©1991 by Falcon Press Publishing Co., Inc., Helena and Billings, Montana

Published in cooperation with the Forest Service, U.S. Department of Agriculture and the Grand Teton Natural History Association.

All rights reserved, including the right to reproduce this book in any form, except brief quotations for reviews, without the written permission of the publisher.

Design, typesetting and other prepress work by Falcon Press, Helena, Montana. Printed in Korea.

Library of Congress Number 90-55079

ISBN 1-56044-020-1

Front cover photo: Cirque of the Towers in the Popo Agie Wilderness, Shoshone National Forest. PAT O'HARA

Back cover photos: fisherman in the Absaroka-Beartooth Wilderness, Custer National Forest. LINDA CAUBLE; fall colors along the Snake River, Targhee National Forest. HOWARD PHOTOGRAPHY; great gray owl in the Bridger-Teton National Forest. DIANA STRATTON

Title page photo: Teton Wilderness, Bridger-Teton National Forest. PAT O'HARA

For additional copies of this book, please check with your local bookstore, or write to Falcon Press, P.O. Box 1718, Helena, MT 59624. To order by phone, call toll-free 1-800-582-2665.

Contents

GREATER YELLOWSTONE NATIONAL FORESTS

The majestic peaks of the Wind River Range dwarf the tents of a base camp set up in lower Titcomb Basin on the Bridger-Teton National Forest. Glaciers carved this range, creating rugged and breathtaking mountains that draw mountaineers and rock climbers. Many of the mountains in the Wind River Range stretch above 12,000 feet. JOHN P. GEORGE

Introduction

A region without borders

*G*reater Yellowstone. In 1917, writer-naturalist Emerson Hough introduced the notion of "Greater Yellowstone" when he appealed for an expansion of Yellowstone National Park. Hough, whose evocative concept was portrayed in *The Saturday Evening Post*, called attention to the interrelated nature of the lands inside and out of the national park boundary. The peerless surroundings that Hough sought for annexation to Yellowstone are today managed by the Forest Service. While the campaign to radically enlarge Yellowstone Park has faded, support for protecting Hough's Greater Yellowstone as a single region has assumed global dimensions.

At the corner of Montana, Idaho, and Wyoming, six national forests team up with Yellowstone National Park to forge a dynamic mosaic of lush coniferous woods, sagebrush meadows, and clear blue lakes and streams. This region — with its abundant wildlife, breathtaking scenery, and rich natural resources — transcends the man-made boundaries that have been imposed upon it. The varied resources are so interrelated that the region has come to be known as the Greater Yellowstone area.

Most people envisioning this region naturally think of Yellowstone National Park, a wonderland of steamy geysers and wild animals. They may also think of neighboring Grand Teton National Park. But those two national parks make up only a portion of Greater

Arrowleaf balsamroot and sticky geraniums carpet a section of the Bridger-Teton National Forest in Wyoming, one of six national forests in the Greater Yellowstone area. GLENN VAN NIMWEGEN

Yellowstone's twelve million acres.

A constellation of six national forests — the Bridger-Teton, Targhee, Gallatin, Shoshone, Beaverhead, and Custer — rims these heralded sanctuaries to complete the Greater Yellowstone. And each of these national forests rivals the national parks in scenic beauty, dramatic topographical features, and cultural history.

Over the centuries, ice, water, wind, lava, earthquakes, and fires have molded the national forests and created landscapes of profound grandeur, crowned by a dozen noble mountain ranges endowed with incomparable vistas. These lands offer the highest point in Wyoming — 13,804-foot Gannett Peak — and the highest point in Montana — 12,799-foot Granite Peak. They also contain one of the world's largest volcanic craters, the Island Park Caldera. They are rich in natural resources as well, containing 1.5 million acres suitable for logging, one of only three known deposits of platinum and palladium in the world, and the largest deposit of chromium ore in the Western Hemisphere.

While they share many common characteristics, the national forests also can claim their own unique features. The Shoshone is the oldest national forest in America. The Bridger-Teton is the second-largest national forest in the lower forty-eight states. The Gallatin holds three famous rivers. The Custer is a high-altitude treasure of minerals and breathtaking views, while the Targhee is nationally known for its abundant and diverse wildlife populations, and the Beaverhead is cattle country.

These national forests got their start in March 1891, when Congress created the Yellowstone Park Timberland Reserve, setting aside roughly 1.25 million acres outside Yellowstone National Park. Many lawmakers at the time saw the forest reserves as a way of preventing abuses such as those that occurred in the East, where hillsides were ravaged by deforestation and mining. To them, the public lands of the West represented the future.

A white-tailed ptarmigan, above, makes its home in the high mountains of the Custer National Forest. This ptarmigan is the only one of the species to sport an all-white tail when its feathers change color in the winter months. MICHAEL S. SAMPLE

Outdoorsmen such as Theodore Roosevelt, who acquired a lasting love for the Greater Yellowstone, argued that only thoughtful care and cultivation of natural resources would preserve the value of the lands. That philosophical legacy continues today on the six national forests of the Greater Yellowstone, where the Forest Service's "multiple-use" approach to management allows for resource development, including recreation, and protection of important features.

However, land managers have closely coordinated multiple use activities in recent years with the national parks, in recognition of the interrelated nature of the land and wildlife of the national forests and the national parks they border. During the 1960s, managers from the six national forests and the two national parks formed the Greater Yellowstone Coordinating Committee, to coordinate management activities among the adjoining units.

A hiker gazes out over the icy waters of Pine Creek Lake and the snowy reaches of 10,941-foot Black Mountain in the Absaroka-Beartooth Wilderness. Pine Creek Lake is on the Gallatin National Forest southeast of Livingston, Montana. HARRY ENGELS

Dawn brings the sun to Bridger-Teton National Forest and an angler to the outlet of Brooks Lake. Fishing is a popular activity on all the national forests of Greater Yellowstone. ERWIN AND PEGGY BAUER

The national forests, administered by the U.S. Department of Agriculture, report to three different regional offices — Ogden, Utah; Missoula, Montana; and Denver, Colorado. The two national parks fall under the jurisdiction of the U.S. Department of the Interior, reporting to the regional office in Denver.

Some conservation groups consider the ecosystem to encompass even more land. But the coordinated management efforts of recent decades recognize the area's common topographical and biological features. For example, diverse habitats stretching for hundreds of miles across national parks and national forests determine the migration patterns of wildlife. Major watersheds often begin in one jurisdiction and pass through another. Forest fires, a phenomenon so forcefully displayed in 1988, race through stands of trees without regard for lines on a map.

Perhaps the argument could be made that each national forest actually contains hundreds, if not thousands, of mini-ecosystems. Together, these smaller parts form Greater Yellowstone, considered by international scientists to be the largest intact ecosystem in the temperate climate zones of the Earth.

The region contains an estimated 1,700 species of vascular plants, 7 percent of which are considered rare and some of which are federally protected. It also boasts at least 12,000 species of insects and 337 species of mammals, birds, and fish — including every large mammal in the western United States except the woodland caribou and the gray wolf. Three national wildlife refuges also provide range for elk, bison, trumpeter swans, whooping cranes, and dozens of other species. Proposals to restore wolves to the region have been made, but no decision has been reached.

In his classic, *A Sand County Almanac*, Aldo Leopold pointed to the national forests of Greater Yellowstone when he wrote that national parks alone cannot protect animals that depend upon vast tracts of land for survival. "The most feasible way to enlarge the area available for wilderness fauna is for the wilder parts of the national forests, which usually surround the parks, to function as parks in respect to threatened species," he said prophetically in 1949.

This prediction can be seen at work in the Greater Yellowstone area, where winter lasts for seven or eight months in the high country. Beginning in late October, deep snows push most wildlife out of the national parks into lower elevations in adjacent national forests. Without adequate winter forage areas, thousands of animals would die of starvation. But the national forests, in cooperation with private land owners, have worked to ensure that winter range is available. Such multi-agency management plans have set a standard for wildlife winter range programs nationwide.

The Greater Yellowstone area provides critical habitat for a number of animals, including the grizzly bear. The area is one of only three remaining grizzly strongholds in the forty-eight contiguous states, and 40 percent of the best grizzly bear range lies in the national forests outside of Yellowstone Park. These forests also contain 55 percent of the newly transplanted peregrine falcons, 60 percent of the trumpeter swans, and 35 percent of the resident bald eagles. And no other region in the country holds a larger concentration of big game animals than does Greater Yellowstone, with its estimated 87,000 mule deer, 68,000 elk, 7,000 bighorn sheep, 6,000 moose, 4,500 antelope, 3,000 black bear, and 1,500 mountain goats. Needless to say, the area is a mecca for hunters and wildlife photographers.

But the region serves other constituencies, as well.

"Conservation," wrote pioneering forester Gifford Pinchot in *Breaking New Ground*, "is the foresighted utilization, preservation, and/or renewal of forests, water, lands, and minerals, for the greatest good of the greatest number in the long run." Those words have been heeded in Greater Yellowstone's national forests.

Stands of lodgepole pine, Douglas-fir, and Engelmann spruce are harvested annually to provide timber for homes. Veins of gold, copper, platinum, and palladium supply valuable minerals for products ranging from jewelry to pollution control devices in automobiles. Untapped reserves of oil and natural gas are seen as a way to decrease America's dependency on foreign crude. And the verdant slopes of grass feed thousands of cattle and sheep each summer. A powerful bond exists between local citizens and the natural resource industries.

But regional economies are shifting away from sole reliance on such jobs. Tourism and recreation are becoming increasingly important industries in the Idaho towns of Ashton, Island Park, and Driggs, the Montana communities of Bozeman, West Yellowstone, Cooke City, Big Timber, and Livingston, and the Wyoming towns of Jackson, Pinedale, Dubois, Lander, and Cody.

Many backcountry enthusiasts are drawn to the twelve wilderness areas that sprawl across Greater Yellowstone. Over 40 percent, or more than four million acres, of the national forests have been designated wilderness and are thus free of most resource development. "A wilderness, in contrast with these acres where man and his own works dominate the landscape, is hereby recognized as an area where the earth and its community of life are untrammeled by man, where man himself is a visitor who does not remain," reads the charter statement of the Wilderness Act of 1964.

Both in and outside of wilderness areas, the national forests contain numerous recreational opportunities for visitors. They have enough miles of hiking trail to reach from Los Angeles to New York City two and a half times, along with campgrounds, lakes, and reservoirs for water sports and streams for fishing.

The pristine headwaters of four major river systems bob and weave through Greater Yellowstone's national forests, gathering momentum from underground springs, melting glaciers, and chutes of mountain run-off. The Yellowstone, Snake, and Green rivers tumble away from the ecosystem and meet the Missouri, Columbia, and Colorado rivers hundreds of miles downstream. The North Platte meanders on its own solitary course into the heartland. From these and about a half dozen secondary drainages, the region exports clean water worth an estimated $250 million in municipal and industrial use.

The rivers also serve as lifelines for plants and animals that depend upon stable stream flows and persistent moisture. And they hold one of Greater

A campfire fends off the approaching dusk, as two backpackers rest at their camp near Soda Lake in the Gros Ventre Mountains, on the Bridger-Teton National Forest. Primitive conditions in this area are the rule, rather than the exception. HENRY HOLDSWORTH

Slide Creek collects the evening shadows as it gently meanders through the Wind River Range in the Bridger Wilderness. The mountain range, marked by sheer rock peaks, also contains glaciers and hundreds of alpine lakes.
JOHN P. GEORGE

Yellowstone's most renowned residents, the trout. Five common species of trout — cutthroats, browns, rainbows, brooks, and lake — can be found here, along with rare golden trout and arctic grayling. As part of the national Rise To The Future program, the six national forests are engaged in preserving spawning habitat and water quality.

Throughout the years, a notable cadre of artists, naturalists, and explorers — including Pinchot, Roosevelt, Leopold, John Muir, Thomas Moran, William Henry Jackson, and Horace Albright — have gained inspiration from the natural resources of Greater Yellowstone. So have numerous visitors who have found peace and tranquility as they pass quietly through the woods and beneath the jagged mountain peaks. It could be argued, perhaps, that no other region in the country offers a better complement of public lands. ∎

The ramparts of Beartooth Butte in the Shoshone National Forest are matched in elegance by the waters of Beartooth Lake, which hugs its base. Visitors camping on the lake's shores may be greeted by elk, deer, moose, or even bald eagles that have been known to prey on unsuspecting trout. MICHAEL S. SAMPLE

Shoshone

Dramatic beauty and history

From its rolling stands of coniferous trees to the moody rapture of its sagebrush-covered badlands, the Shoshone National Forest has a flavor all its own. Some might argue the Shoshone derives its elegance from the sheer drama of its geography. Others might say the national forest is enriched by its history. Either way, its attributes are remarkable.

Tucked between the eastern edge of Yellowstone National Park and the rugged plains of northwest Wyoming, the 2.4 million-acre Shoshone was the nation's first national forest. And it remains today a living symbol of man's compatibility with a natural environment.

On March 3, 1891, Congress set aside roughly 1.25 million acres east of Yellowstone Park as the "Yellowstone Park Timberland Reserve," to ensure protection and wise use of the region's rich natural resources. Just sixteen years later, a major portion of this reserve became the nucleus of the Shoshone, considered a model for the national forest system.

Filled with more than 1,000 miles of rivers, 1,300 miles of inventoried hiking trails, and 1,500 miles of roads, this spacious wildland offers diverse avenues to rustic tranquility.

A century ago, William F. "Buffalo Bill" Cody so fancied these forest lands that he frequently hunted and sought solace among the glorious stands of pine and subalpine fir. Eventually, the legendary

frontiersman founded a community east of the current national forest boundary. Today, the town that bears his name — Cody, Wyoming — also contains the national forest headquarters. Cody contains, as well, the Buffalo Bill Historical Center, which features the famed outdoorsman's memorabilia, along with old photographs of the national forest.

The legacy of Buffalo Bill is ingrained into many aspects of the Shoshone. Just outside Yellowstone's east gate along U.S. highways 14/16/20, Buffalo Bill's historic hunting lodge — Pahaska Tepee — serves as a gateway to the North Absaroka Wilderness. In 1913, Cody led the king of Monaco on a hunting trip into the wilderness along the Pahaska-Sunlight Trail. A memento of that adventure still stands. At Camp Monaco, a member of the hunting group carved a scene into a giant spruce and left behind the name "Camp Monaco." Although the spruce was killed by the Clover-Mist forest fire in 1988, national forest historians are con-

The setting moon hovers over the Beartooth Mountains. This view was captured near the Beartooth Highway, a national forest scenic byway that crosses a portion of the Shoshone as it connects the Montana towns of Cooke City and Red Lodge. MICHAEL S. SAMPLE

sidering ways to permanently preserve the landmark.

Visitors traveling to Yellowstone National Park from Cody can view another piece of history from the earliest days of the national forest system. The log Wapiti Ranger Station along U.S. highways 14/16/20 was the first Forest Service structure built with government funds, between 1903 and 1905. It served as an administrative base for the Yellowstone Park Timberland Reserve and is still used by rangers today.

For the hiker or horseback rider immersed in the backcountry, the landscape recalls an era when thousands of bison roamed free and adventurers such as

Cody launched grand expeditions into the wild frontier. Lofty peaks rising from the Absaroka, Beartooth, and Wind River ranges dominate the horizon almost anywhere on the Shoshone. Fully 25 percent of the national forest lies above timberline, marked by high-elevation plateaus, glacial cirques, and saw-toothed ridges.

Fifty-five percent of the Shoshone remains wild today, set aside in five federally designated wilderness areas — more than any other national forest in the tri-state region of Idaho, Montana, and Wyoming.

Recreationists pack into the backcountry on horses along Bears Ears Trail in the Wind River Range. Scenes such as this reflect the Shoshone's cowboy heritage. Everyone from Cub Scouts to well-known diplomats have saddled up and trotted into the backcountry of northwest Wyoming. GEORGE WUERTHNER

The 704,529-acre Washakie Wilderness is the Shoshone's largest, abutting the entire southeast corner of Yellowstone National Park. Named for Chief Washakie of the Shoshone Indian tribe, the wilderness contains remnants of petrified forests, as well as superb hunting and fishing opportunities that attract sportsmen from around the globe.

The North Absaroka Wilderness covers 350,488 acres along the northeastern border of Yellowstone Park. And on the far northern tier of the Shoshone, where Wyoming meets the Montana border, the national forest manages 23,750 acres of the massive Absaroka-Beartooth Wilderness. The Gallatin and Custer national forests in Montana share administration of the 945,000-acre Absaroka-Beartooth, which is nearly 100 miles long.

Snowcapped for much of the year, the region around the Absaroka-Beartooth Wilderness contains active glaciers and high-elevation plateaus. Sculptors of

Indian paintbrush and lupines dress the base of the Warbonnet, Warrior I, and Warrior II peaks in the Popo Agie Wilderness in the Shoshone National Forest. These steep mountains make up one facet of Cirque of the Towers, a popular hiking and climbing destination. JEFF GNASS

mountains, the glaciers are reminders of Ice Age effects on this area 12,000 years ago. The slow-moving ice fields left behind a panorama of cirque bowls and terminal moraine slopes.

Sprawled across the southern Absarokas and the mighty Wind River mountains are two smaller wilderness areas known for their superb trout fishing and rock climbing. The 198,838-acre Fitzpatrick and the 101,991-acre Popo Agie wilderness areas — characterized by steep and strenuous terrain — offer the best views in all of west-central Wyoming.

As the high mountain peaks attest, geology has

A least chipmunk nibbles on a pine cone. Its diet usually consists of seeds, fruits, berries, and grasses, but it will investigate opportunities at campgrounds and picnic areas. The Shoshone harbors mammals from the tiny size of chipmunks to the powerful bulk of moose and grizzly bears.
TIM FITZHARRIS

played an important role in shaping the Shoshone. And the same processes that forged mountains and valleys left behind a vast wealth of minerals and oil. Beneath the soil of the Shoshone lies a small portion of a geologic formation known as the Overthrust Belt, believed to extend from Mexico to Canada. Trapped within this geologic feature are thought to be millions, if not billions, of dollars worth of oil and natural gas. Oil and gas companies hold leases on approximately 390,000 acres of the Shoshone that straddle the Overthrust Belt.

These hills also hold gold. Under an 1872 mining law, almost one million acres of the Shoshone are available for exploration and possible mining of hardrock minerals. Active mining claims still remain, mostly for gold and silver.

A century ago, the buckled hills northwest of Lander saw a flurry of gold mining that created a half dozen mining boom towns. Visitors driving south of Lander near South Pass, off Wyoming Highway 28, will see the wooden skeletons of ghost towns — a haunting reminder of the Shoshone's gold rush heritage.

While the national forests of the region also yield

A sheepherder stands outside the tiny camp trailer he calls home while tending sheep as they graze on the lush grasses of the Shoshone. The grasslands also support cattle and horses. GREG L. RYAN AND SALLY A. BEYER

millions of board feet of timber for homes and other wood products, much of the timberland in the Shoshone is found on steep slopes. Only about 4 percent is available for logging. Thus when timber companies finished cutting trees in flat sections, little of the national forest remained to meet timber demands. Mills such as the Louisiana-Pacific in Dubois have shut down in recent years. But that small community has rebounded by emphasizing tourism, recreation, and hunting. All three of those industries are Shoshone trademarks.

About 27,000 cattle, sheep, and horses graze the Shoshone high country today — a level far lower than the 150,000 animals that grazed at the turn of the century. By trimming that number over the last four decades, the Shoshone has tried to reduce the effects of livestock on watersheds and forage.

The Shoshone is a premier habitat for the approximately 200 grizzlies in the Greater Yellowstone ecosystem. By September, grizzlies leave the high country solitude after gorging themselves on a favorite snack — whitebark pine nuts. The Shoshone contains more whitebark pine trees than any other national

Winter makes a stark backdrop for this pack of howling coyotes, top, in the Shoshone National Forest. JEFFREY T. HOGAN

Perfect symmetry characterizes the Rocky Mountain iris, left, a delicate dweller of river bottoms and moist meadows within the Shoshone National Forest. The flower's sweet fragrance attracts bees that collect its nectar to make honey. MICHAEL S. SAMPLE

SCENIC SPLENDOR BY ROAD OR TRAIL

Snowmobilers find ideal conditions on many of the national forests in the Greater Yellowstone area. The Shoshone holds portions of the proposed Continental Divide Snowmobile Trail, designed to cover 350 miles as it links Lander, Wyoming, with Yellowstone National Park. TIM EGAN

Whether traveling by car in the summer or snowmobile in the winter, visitors to the Shoshone National Forest have a bounty of scenic routes from which to choose.

Snowmobilers have access to one of the longest trail systems in the world — the proposed Continental Divide Snowmobile Trail, devised by a group of Lander residents, the Forest Service, the National Park Service, and the state of Wyoming. This route begins outside of Lander, Wyoming, traverses the Shoshone and Bridger-Teton national forests, and connects with groomed trails at the south entrance of Yellowstone National Park.

Extending for 350 miles, the trail allows snowmobilers to experience some of the finest scenery in the northern Rockies. In a single trip, visitors can see the Wind River, Absaroka, Teton, and Madison mountain ranges, key fixtures of the Continental Divide. The trail

veers northwest from Lander to Pinedale, crosses the Continental Divide, travels on to Dubois, then scales 9,658-foot Togwotee Pass and descends into the breathtaking valley of Jackson Hole. Swinging north, it is designed to cross through a portion of the Grand Teton Park backcountry and arrive at Flagg Ranch in the John D. Rockefeller Parkway. From there, snowmobilers can enter the south gate of Yellowstone and link up with more than 1,500 miles of trails in eastern Idaho and southern Montana.

During the summer, motorists can choose from three highways virtually custom-made for the scenic connoisseur.

The Wyoming Scenic Centennial Byway honors the state's 100th birthday and takes travelers over Togwotee Pass (U.S. Highway 26/287) from Dubois. The route offers stunning views of the Absaroka and Teton ranges, then swings south via U.S. 189/191 to Pinedale.

The recently designated Beartooth National Forest Scenic Byway (U.S. Highway 212) is one of the most scenic drives in the country. Connecting the Montana towns of Cooke City and Red Lodge, the road crosses the Shoshone and Custer national forests as it ascends the astounding heights of 10,936-foot Beartooth Pass. The road offers many opportunties for spotting wildlife.

The Chief Joseph Scenic Highway (Wyoming Highway 296) veers off Wyoming 120 to connect Cody with the Beartooth byway. This is one of the wildest corridors of the Shoshone National Forest, providing access to the famed Clarks Fork of the Yellowstone River and Sunlight Basin. From this rustic pastoral highway, visitors can explore trout streams and take in wondrous views of Pilot and Index peaks.

Bighorn sheep dot the Whiskey Mountain Winter Range, just outside of Dubois. Between 900 and 1,100 sheep winter here each year. The range is the largest winter range area for bighorn sheep in the forty-eight contiguous states. Sheep from here are often transplanted to other areas in Wyoming and neighboring states. JEFF VANUGA

forest in Greater Yellowstone.

At least 337 species of mammals, birds, and fish have established niches in the Shoshone. When the summer sun soaks the higher elevations, snow rapidly retreats and leaves behind meadows bursting with wildflowers. Grizzlies, black bears, elk, bighorn sheep, mountain lions, deer, and Rocky Mountain goats wander through vast glades of wildflowers. Along the lush banks of the Shoshone, Wood, Clarks Fork, and Wind rivers, wildlife watchers will find an astonishing assortment of plants and animals. From June to November, hunters and anglers descend upon the national forest. Forty-eight species of fish and wildlife are classified as game animals for hunting and angling purposes.

Compared to other national forests in the Greater Yellowstone region, the Shoshone contains the largest amount of summer range for bighorn sheep, elk, and mule deer. It also has more moose habitat than the six other national forests combined.

During the winter, thousands of elk and mule deer leave the higher elevations in Yellowstone National Park in search of lowland grazing areas on the Shoshone National Forest. Because many of these areas outside the national park are privately owned and have been developed, river bottoms on the national forest are vital to these species during the harsh winter months. Elk and deer commonly migrate into the country around the North Fork of the Shoshone River and the Sunlight Basin area south of the Clarks Fork of the Yellowstone River.

Remote pockets of the Shoshone provide a haven for a number of federally protected species that have been classified rare, endangered, or threatened. In addition to grizzlies, the national forest offers at least seasonal habitat for bald eagles, peregrine falcons, and trumpeter swans. Whenever a new development is proposed, foresters consider the potential impact on key "indicator species" — such as wolverines, lynx, rare trout, and goshawk — in certain habitats.

In recent years, meadowlands adjacent to the Shoshone have been targeted as recovery sites for the endangered black-footed ferret. During the 1980s, the last known black-footed ferrets were discovered less than five air miles from the eastern edge of the national forest, near the town of Meeteetse, Wyoming. Fearing the species was dangerously close to extinction, researchers collected the remaining ferrets from their burrows and began a captive breeding program that has met with great success.

While the Shoshone annually records one million visitor days, recreation use is far below the national average. Backcountry trails lend themselves to solitude, and wildlife watchers can see the newest crop of animals in the spring and elk bugling in the autumn.

The Clarks Fork River of the Yellowstone, located between the Absaroka-Beartooth and North Absaroka wilderness areas, captures the awesome power of nature. Named for explorer William Clark, the river crashes through a canyon whose walls climb 1,200 feet above the thunderous whitewater. The river drops an average of 100 feet per mile as it enters Wyoming's deepest gorge, northeast of the Sunlight Basin area. Only expert kayakers have attempted to run its seemingly unnavigable bounty of rapids.

Designated as Wyoming's first federal Wild and Scenic River, the Clarks Fork contains spectacular vistas for recreationists and sportsmen. Information on camping, fishing, and hunting opportunities is available at the Clarks Fork Ranger District Office.

In 1988, forest fires burned out of Yellowstone Park and passed through this area, leaving more than 120,000 acres of hillsides blackened with charcoal snags. Al-

A cross-country skier, above, pauses in the crisp winter air as a gray jay perches on her hat. The Shoshone, like the other national forests of Greater Yellowstone, offers miles of both groomed and untracked nordic skiing. W. PERRY CONWAY

Clear, cool Horse Creek meanders through the center of the Shoshone, left. The trout-filled stream offers a dazzling view of the Absaroka Mountains and diverse wildlife habitat. JEFF VANUGA

Weathered tree stumps stand out at Cirque of the Towers, a rugged area that straddles the Continental Divide. Located in the Popo Agie Wilderness, Cirque of the Towers contains a number of lakes and 12,000-foot mountains. PAT O'HARA

ready, the burned trees are providing habitat for cavity-nesting birds and funneling important nutrients into the soil. Forest Service rehabilitation projects have salvaged some of the burned timber and reseeded or reforested parts of the burned area. As the forest regenerates, hikers and sportsmen will witness one of the most profound metamorphoses of nature's beauty.

For the winter sports enthusiast, the Shoshone offers miles of powder-rich terrain for snowmobilers and skiers. The Clarks Fork Snowmobile Trail runs parallel to the Chief Joseph Highway (Wyoming Highway 296) and joins with a trail system leading to Cooke City, Montana. The proposed Continental Divide Snowmobile Trail is one of the longest groomed trails in the world.

As visitors tour the Shoshone, they will discover that the beauty of its wild landscape speaks for itself. The Shoshone was the first national forest, and many would argue it is also the best. ∎

Bridal Veil Falls in the Clarks Fork Canyon, cascades over weather-worn rock formed millions of years ago. JOHN R. BOEHMKE

Broad valleys unfold before the high reaches of the
Beartooth Range, above. The Shoshone National Forest
shares the Beartooth Range — and portions of the
related Absaroka-Beartooth Wilderness — with the
Custer National Forest in Montana. JEFF VANUGA

Alpine and nordic skiers consider the marbled face of
Brooks Mountain an ideal spot for touring the Shoshone
and adjacent Bridger-Teton national forests. Here, a
plucky visitor tests the aerodynamics of his cross-country
skis. JEFF VANUGA

SHOSHONE
NATIONAL FOREST DIRECTORY
GREATER YELLOWSTONE AREA

POINTS OF INTEREST

WAPITI RANGER STATION, located along U.S. Highway 14/16/20 between Yellowstone National Park and Cody, is the first station built with government funds.

PAHASKA TEEPEE, along U.S. 14/16/20, was Buffalo Bill Cody's historic hunting camp. Along the Pahaska-Sunlight Trail are remnants of Camp Monaco, created when Cody and the king of Monaco hunted there nearly a century ago.

BUFFALO BILL RESERVOIR west of Cody along U.S. 14/16/20 is a popular destination for water recreationists.

WILDERNESS AREAS

ABSAROKA-BEARTOOTH 23,750 acres on the Shoshone, in the northern portion of the national forest.

NORTH ABSAROKA 350,488 acres in the northern portion of the Shoshone, along the northeastern border of Yellowstone National Park.

WASHAKIE 704,529 acres in the southern half of the national forest, along the southeastern edge of Yellowstone National Park. Contains petrified forests and excellent hunting and fishing.

FITZPATRICK 198,838 acres in the southern half of the Shoshone.

POPO AGIE 101,991 acres in the southern half of the national forest.

RECREATIONAL OPPORTUNITIES

HIKING AND RIDING Some 1,300 miles of trails are open to both hiking and horseback riding, but check with local ranger stations for possible closures during the spring and fall. Some non-wilderness areas of the forest allow mountain biking. The Continental Divide National Scenic Trail crosses portions of the Shoshone and adjacent Bridger-Teton National Forest.

CAMPING Three dozen main campgrounds around the national forest, with a dozen alone on U.S. Highway 14/16/20 between the east entrance of Yellowstone National Park and Cody.

SCENIC DRIVES The Beartooth National Forest Scenic Byway (U.S. Highway 212), one of the most scenic drives in America, crosses a portion of the Shoshone as it links Cooke City and Red Lodge, Montana. The Chief Joseph Scenic Highway (Wyoming Highway 296) northwest of Cody follows the Clarks Fork of the Yellowstone River and offers excellent opportunities for seeing wildlife. The Wyoming Scenic Centennial Byway west of Dubois on U.S. Highway 26/287 ascends Togwotee Pass.

KAYAKING AND RAFTING Both forks of the Shoshone River provide opportunities for scenic floats. The Clarks Fork of the Yellowstone River offers whitewater kayaking for experts only.

HUNTING Trophy-class elk, moose, mule deer, and bighorn sheep, as well as antelope, waterfowl, and other upland game birds. Licenses required by the Wyoming Game and Fish Department.

FISHING Superb angling for trout on the Clarks Fork of the Yellowstone River, both branches of the Shoshone River, and dozens of other primary and secondary tributaries. Excellent lake fishing in the Wind River Range. Check for special regulations. License required.

CROSS-COUNTRY SKIING Summer hiking trails are available for nordic skiing. Telemark and backcountry skiing is popular, but check avalanche conditions with local ranger stations.

SNOWMOBILING Dozens of trails open to snowmobiling, including the proposed 350-mile Continental Divide Snowmobile Trail between Lander and the south entrance to Yellowstone Park. The Clarks Fork Snowmobile Trail links Cooke City, Montana, with the junction of U.S. Highway 212 and Wyoming Highway 296.

OFF-ROAD VEHICLES Good opportunity for trail bike use along secondary roads and some trails. Check with ranger district for travel management information.

ADMINISTRATIVE OFFICES

FOREST HEADQUARTERS 225 W. Yellowstone Avenue, Cody, WY 82414, (307) 527-6241

CLARKS FORK RANGER DISTRICT 1002 Road 11, Powell, WY 82435, (307) 754-7207

GREYBULL RANGER DISTRICT 2044 State Street, Meeteetse, WY 82433, (307) 868-2379

WAPITI RANGER DISTRICT 203 A Yellowstone, Cody, WY 82414, (307) 527-6921

WIND RIVER RANGER DISTRICT 209 Ramshorn, Dubois, WY 82513, (307) 455-2466

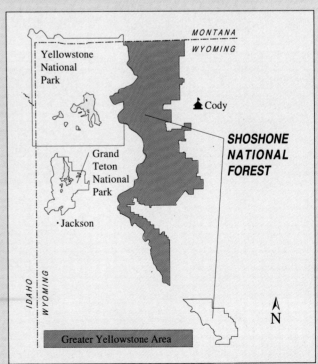

The majestic stump of Squaretop Mountain reaches into the clouds and blue sky. The distinctive 11,695-foot summit is the most photographed peak in the Wind River Range. It attracts a loyal cadre of hikers and mountaineers who often congregate at Green River Lakes Campground eight miles away. ED COOPER

Bridger-Teton

Dazzling mountain splendor

Perhaps no other national forest in the West arouses as much emotion in visitors as the Bridger-Teton National Forest of northwest Wyoming. Among the seven national forests in the Greater Yellowstone area, the Bridger-Teton is the biggest, records the most recreation use, and ranks second in total wilderness acreage.

This 3.4 million-acre national forest stretches from the southern border of Yellowstone National Park into the sagebrush prairies of west-central Wyoming, wrapping around the historic valley of Jackson Hole and embracing the entire eastern flank of Grand Teton National Park. Visitors seek solitude year-round among its tapestry of lakes, forests, and mountains.

The national forest has its headquarters in the Wild West town of Jackson, where the famed elkhorn archways adorn the town square. Both the town and the Bridger-Teton National Forest have strong ties to mountain men such as John Colter, Davey Jackson, and Jim Bridger, who explored the region during the nineteenth century. Perhaps as early as 1819, French-speaking trappers viewed the line of sawtoothed peaks running north and called them the "Trois Tetons," or three breasts. English-speaking mountain men called them "Pilot Knobs," but the French name remained. These spectacular peaks are the core of Grand Teton National Park. Their western flank is on the Targhee National Forest, in the Jedediah Smith Wilderness.

Ferry Lake nestles among the snowy reaches of the Teton Range, in the Teton Wilderness. This rugged wilderness contains many remote areas for those seeking solitude. PAT O'HARA

Glacier-carved peaks in the Gros Ventre and Wind River mountain ranges mark the eastern edge of the Bridger-Teton National Forest. The jagged teeth of the Teton Range and the rounded summits of the Palisades border the western edge. Among the forests and meadows of these ranges winds a trail system spanning 3,000 miles and a network of scenic roads stretching more than 2,500 miles. Streams here nourish five major watersheds — the Snake, Green, Yellowstone, Bear, and Platte.

The Bridger-Teton also holds important natural resources. In the same woods where wildlife managers are trying to protect habitat for grizzly bears, petroleum companies are drilling exploratory wells 13,000 feet deep in an attempt to find pockets of oil and natural gas. The coniferous forests that provide cover for elk and moose also provide timber for homes and paper products. The same rivers that teem with cutthroat trout furnish water to communities and industries

hundreds of miles downstream. To fulfill the many public demands placed upon it, the Bridger-Teton has searched for a balance between preservation and wise use of raw materials.

The national forest records nearly two million visitor days each year. Although many people are passing through on their way to the adjacent national parks, the Bridger-Teton itself has much to offer.

The national forest contains three splendid wilderness areas — the Bridger, the Teton, and the Gros Ventre. These areas cover more than one-third of the national forest and contain critical migration routes for wildlife. Thus they contribute immensely to the region's overall biological diversity. At least seventy-four mammal species and 208 species of birds live in the Bridger-Teton area.

Because of its close proximity to Yellowstone and Grand Teton national parks, the Bridger-Teton is a haven for many rare and federally protected species.

Sightings of grizzly bears, bald eagles, peregrine falcons, wolverines, lynx, trumpeter swans, sandhill and whooping cranes, and osprey occur each year. The mountain toad and three genetically pure subspecies of cutthroat trout — the fine-spotted, Bonneville, and Colorado — also are found here. And near the Green River, the Kendall Warm Springs dace lives in the tepid waters of a spring. This tiny, colorful, and evasive fish is found nowhere else in the world. The national forest has undertaken strict measures to protect the endangered dace and its habitat, which is highly sensitive to disturbance. Visitors to Kendall Warm Springs should use caution and remember that it is illegal to catch or disturb these amazing fish.

The Bridger-Teton also contains every large mammal species in the forty-eight contiguous states except woodland caribou and the once-native gray wolf. During the 1930s, federal bounty hunters eliminated the last of the wolves, which were preying upon domestic cattle and sheep. But efforts have been under way in recent years to bring wolves back to Yellowstone Park. Should reintroduction occur, wildlife in the Bridger-Teton will play an important role in building a strong wolf population. Biologists believe the wolves would prey primarily on elk. The Bridger-Teton's wintering elk population numbers about 22,000 — one of the largest concentrations of elk on public lands.

The national forest also contains 53,000 mule deer, 6,000 moose, 3,500 bighorn sheep, 18,000 antelope, and 6,000 black bear. Numbers alone, however, can be deceiving. The entire Greater Yellowstone region lacks adequate winter habitat for migratory animals such as elk, deer, bighorn sheep, and antelope.

Almost the entire Jackson Hole Valley rests within former wildlife winter range. The town of Jackson and nearby ranches, for example, occupy key meadowlands. Development of these crucial areas caused thousands of elk to starve early in this century. The high number of deaths led to the formation of the National Elk Refuge in 1912, an area that stretches north from Jackson.

Since then, the Bridger-Teton has helped pave the way for wildlife management on the southern front of the Greater Yellowstone area. It has, for example, worked with the Wyoming Game and Fish Department to secure winter range, coordinate hunts, and protect riparian habitat for trout and federally protected bald eagles.

The elk refuge supports 9,400 elk that leave the high country from as far away as Yellowstone Park and

A great gray owl feasts upon a mouse. The owl is one of many raptors found in the Bridger-Teton National Forest. GLENN VAN NIMWEGEN

migrate into Jackson Hole, where they are given supplemental feed. Elsewhere in the Bridger-Teton, the Wyoming Game and Fish Department operates twenty-two feed grounds, many of which allow visitors to see the animals at close range.

Elk and other wildlife in the area — grizzlies, bald eagles, and moose — depend on stable habitat year-round. They need adequate winter range and migration routes, for example. Wildlife managers often point to the Bridger-Teton's three wilderness areas to explain why animal populations are thriving.

Nestled along the southern border of Yellowstone Park and flush with the western face of the Absaroka Range, the Teton Wilderness offers some of the ecosystem's most important habitat for grizzlies and elk. The entire 585,500-acre wilderness rests within a management zone deemed crucial to the survival of the great bears. Roughly 200 grizzlies occupy the Greater

Born of glaciers and snowpacked peaks in the Wind River Range, the Green River is a radiant tributary of the mighty Colorado River. Its gentle riffles are an angler's delight. DAVID MUENCH

Yellowstone area, one of only three regions in the lower forty-eight states with a viable grizzly population. To keep the population strong, untrammeled wildlands such as the Teton Wilderness are needed so the bears can expand their range outside the national park boundaries. The remote terrain and plentiful supply of food are ideal for the powerful bears.

Accented by craggy mountain tops, tundra-like plateaus, broad, sloping valleys, and dense pine forests, the Teton Wilderness also serves as a corridor for thousands of elk migrating between Yellowstone Park and Jackson Hole. As a result, hunters worldwide are drawn to the wilderness every autumn.

While the wilderness landscape appears peaceful, it has witnessed many changes. Near Enos Lake, visitors can see the effects of two profound phenomena —

wind and fire. In 1987, a freak thunderstorm produced the world's highest-elevation tornado, leaving a swath of downed trees stretching more than twenty-one miles in length and two miles in width. Adjacent to the "blowdown area" are blackened snags from a wildfire that roared across the national forest in 1988 and played a key role in the historic fire season in and around Yellowstone Park.

The Huckleberry Mountain Fire Lookout stands at the western border of the wilderness. This last remaining structure from the days of manned fire lookouts is no longer used, but is protected as a national historic site. Farther east, hikers will find ambling rivers around the Two Ocean Plateau National Natural Area, also known as Parting of the Waters Area. The area, designated in 1965, was named for the Atlantic Creek and

Pacific Creek drainages that flow toward their namesake oceans.

The 287,000-acre Gros Ventre Wilderness, named for an Indian tribe that once roamed the Bridger-Teton, is located in the heart of the national forest. This land of speckled lakes and lush river bottoms is a mecca for backpackers, horseback riders, and hunters. From the valley floor of Jackson Hole, the wilderness area's western slopes tower above the National Elk Refuge and Grand Teton National Park. Jackson Peak, with its sheer north face, looms near a geologic feature fondly known by local residents as the "Sleeping Indian," officially called Sheep Mountain. With only a little imagination, it's easy to spot an Indian chief lying in repose, his headdress pointing to the south and his legs extending to the north. The rolling buttresses of the

Broken tree trunks stand as a reminder of the forces of nature. Trees in a 21-mile stretch of the Teton Wilderness were downed during a 1987 tornado. JEFF VANUGA

Gros Ventre Range and popular destinations such as Goodwin Lake and Ouzel Falls lie behind this steep facade.

The third, and arguably most dramatic, wilderness is the 428,200-acre Bridger Wilderness. During the 1980s, a public campaign was launched to turn part of the wilderness into a national park because of its stately beauty. The effort was temporarily derailed, however, when citizens learned that national park status might require development and road building at the breathtaking base of the Wind River mountains. Often compared to the Swiss Alps, the Wind River Range contains a collection of 10,000-year-old glaciers, more than 1,200 alpine lakes, and numerous sheer granite peaks. The mountain community of Pinedale is a recreational center, and the Pinedale Ranger District is the logical starting point for trips into the wilderness.

Dominated by 12,000-foot peaks, the Wind River Range holds 13,804-foot Gannett Peak, the highest point in Wyoming. This awesome summit, thirty-four feet taller than the Grand Teton, was named after Henry Gannett, who helped map the region a century ago. Nearby is the second-highest point in the Wind River Range — 13,745-foot Fremont Peak, honoring Western explorer John C. Fremont.

In the southern reaches of the range lies Cirque of the Towers and in the north, Titcomb Basin. Both attract mountaineers and rock climbers who scramble across headwalls once carved by mammoth glaciers. Few of the hikes in this area are flat, and many can be rugged. But dozens of less strenuous trails exist, suitable for day excursions. Because of the area's immense popularity, the national forest closely monitors and manages the trail system and campsites in the Wind Rivers to prevent overuse.

Portions of the Continental Divide National Scenic Trail — considered the gemstone of hiking trails in the Rocky Mountains — cross the northeastern flank of the Bridger-Teton. Some 220 miles of the trail weave across the Teton and Bridger wilderness areas from South Pass to the southern border of Yellowstone Park. The Sheridan National Recreation Trail branches off from this main trail, following a route taken by Lieutenant General Philip H. Sheridan during his Army expedition to Yellowstone in 1881. The Sheridan Trail, roughly sixteen miles long, extends from the adjacent Shoshone National Forest boundary to Breakneck Creek in the Gros Ventre River drainage.

The southern half of the national forest, marked by

Portions of the Jedediah Smith Wilderness on the Targhee National Forest offer hikers a breathtaking view of the Bridger-Teton National Forest and the outstanding pinnacles of the Teton Range. The wilderness was named after legendary mountain man Jedediah Smith. RALPH MAUGHAN

dense carpets of trees and broad expanses of sky, contains a cache of natural wonders. While much of the area lies outside of Greater Yellowstone, visitors may want to take note of some of its features.

Just outside of Afton at the end of Swift Creek road is a little-known feature called Periodic Springs, one of only a handful of cold water geysers in the word. It's fed by a chilly reservoir, in contrast to the geothermal features of such geysers as Old Faithful in Yellowstone Park.

A line of auburn cliffs known as the "Red Castles" runs about seven miles north of Big Piney Creek and six miles south of South Cotton Creek. These fiery-colored rocks present a fortress-like appearance.

Two lakes in the southern portion of the national forest are also popular with visitors. Lake Alice, with its backdrop of mountains, offers angling and hiking opportunities. And Middle Piney Lake is known for its high-elevation boating and camping.

A bounty of natural resources has turned national forest management into a sensitive balancing act, as questions are raised over the appropriate role of oil and natural gas exploration, logging, and livestock grazing. The Bridger-Teton is a national leader in regulating development to reduce the impact on the environment.

Oil and gas development is one example. Scientists believe portions of a huge geologic formation called the "Overthrust Belt" — a mixture of sedimentary rock that has trapped large pockets of oil and gas — lie beneath the Bridger-Teton. The belt may be as large as sixty miles wide and may extend from Canada to Mexico, containing up to fifteen billion barrels of oil and sixty-five trillion cubic feet of natural gas. The potential for a large find has spurred interest in exploration.

Oil and gas development is prohibited in wilderness areas. But roughly 95 percent of the remaining acreage in the national forest, or approximately 1.8 million acres, is open to leasing and exploration. Because of the steep slopes and unstable soils in much of the

Ringed by 10,000-year-old glaciers, Cirque of the Towers in the Bridger Wilderness is a popular haven for rock climbers and alpine backpackers. Wildflowers accent the craggy environs during the summer months.
DAVID MUENCH

ENJOYING A WINTER WONDERLAND

Winter can last six months on the national forests of the Greater Yellowstone area, where snowfall is measured in feet rather than inches. The Bridger-Teton National Forest represents a wonderland for skiers and snowmobilers, who will find numerous recreational opportunities within easy reach.

The sixty-four-run Jackson Hole Ski Area — a household word in downhill skiing — sprawls across the face of Rendezvous Mountain on national forest land. Its vertical drop is more than 4,000 feet, the greatest of any slope in the continental United States. An aerial tram carries skiers to the top of Rendezvous Peak, where they can find fresh snow almost daily, along with an arresting view of the valley below. Jackson Hole's popularity is proven by figures: it records 250,000 skier days a year. Summer visitors come as well, to ride the tram and see the spectacular views and flowers on top of Rendezvous Mountain.

The ski area is based at Teton Village, Wyoming, about a twenty-minute drive from downtown Jackson.

Skiers can hit the slopes even closer to Jackson, too. The Snow King Ski Area is located just six blocks from the Jackson town square and covers 400 acres on the Bridger-Teton. It offers 1,571 feet of vertical terrain, a northern exposure, two chairlifts, and twelve runs for skiers of all ability levels. Snow King — Wyoming's first ski resort, built in 1939 — records about 75,000 skier days annually. Chairlifts to the top of Snow King Mountain run throughout the summer and provide hikers and mountain bikers with access to the national forest.

Skiing "the pass" is a popular activity in Jackson Hole, and for good reason. The Teton Pass Road, connecting Wyoming with Idaho, climbs to 8,431 feet. Skiers revel in the snow conditions found here. TOM BEAN

Downhill skiing can be found outside developed areas, as well. Teton Pass, Cache Creek, Phillips Canyon, and Togwotee Pass all offer a multitude of options for downhill skiers, telemarkers, and snowboarders, who should check snow conditions with the Wyoming Highway Department. Winter recreationists also should be mindful of avalanche danger, which can be checked with the Forest Service by calling (307) 733-2664.

Helicopter skiing also has grown in popularity during recent years, and independent helicopter operators ferry skiers to remote slopes for untracked powder and stunning views.

Cross-country skiing and snowmobiling are allowed along much of the Bridger-Teton trail system, although snowmobiles are not allowed in wilderness areas. Snowmobilers also can haul their machines to the northern portion of the national forest and Grand Teton National Park, to connect with a trail system that winds across unplowed roads in Yellowstone National Park and leads to hundreds of miles of trails at West Yellowstone, Montana. Or they can travel to the heated waters at Granite Hot Springs resort near the banks of Granite Creek, southeast of Jackson via U.S. Highway 189. The area is also open to summer visitors and can be reached by taking the Granite Creek Road nine miles from the Battle Mountain turnoff on U.S. 189.

Groomed trails also can be found on Blackrock Creek by Togwotee Mountain Lodge. Other popular snowmobile areas include the Gros Ventre Road, Greys River Road, and Upper Green River.

national forest, the Forest Service has required exhaustive measures to minimize the effects of drilling and road building in remote areas. The oil and gas industry has probed to great depths to find commercial quantities, often drilling 13,000 feet and deeper. One exploratory well in the Bridger-Teton was drilled to 22,000 feet, or more than four miles in depth — among the deepest wells ever drilled in the country. So far, companies have failed to find quantities of oil or gas that would warrant full-field development in the Jackson area, but extensive natural gas development has occurred in the Riley Ridge area near Big Piney.

Conservationists have sought to ban all exploration on the national forest, citing the Bridger-Teton's ecological importance to wildlife. They fear the consequences of development if commercial amounts of natural fuel are found. One area of concern is 10,326-foot Mount Leidy, a pyramid-shaped peak surrounded by highlands that harbor grizzly bears. The Mount Leidy area, near the border of Grand Teton National Park, has not yielded large supplies of oil or gas. But conservationists say development here is incompatible with Jackson Hole's tourism and recreation industries.

Two federal laws pertaining to oil and gas govern the Forest Service on this issue. The Energy Security Act promotes exploration on public lands to help make the United States less dependent on foreign fuel. The National Environmental Policy Act, meanwhile, prohibits development that may cause environmental degradation. The resolution of these conflicting goals in the Bridger-Teton could set the standard for similar resource development in other national forests.

Oil and gas are only two of the natural resources on the Bridger-Teton. Pine, spruce, and

Summer visitors to the Bridger-Teton National Forest are greeted by an eruption of wildflowers each summer. The reddish hues of Indian paintbrush are common across the sub-alpine slopes. MICHAEL S. SAMPLE

The Teton Wilderness cradles the headwaters of the Yellowstone River, top, which flows north through Yellowstone National Park into Montana. TOM MURPHY

subalpine fir have long supported an active logging industry. But Bridger-Teton managers have reduced the annual yield to focus on preserving wildlife habitat and scenic vistas. The region's harsh climate makes planting and revegetation extremely difficult. About twelve million board feet of timber is slated to be cut annually over the next twenty years, representing a 70 percent decrease in production from the thirty million board feet cut annually in the 1980s.

Ranchers also have left their mark on Wyoming, which is nicknamed "the Cowboy State," and the Bridger-Teton contains some of the richest grazing lands in the state. The Upper Green River cattle allotment, which provides grass for thousands of cattle, is the largest single livestock allotment in the entire national forest system. More than 40,000 cattle, 80,000 sheep, and 2,000 horses graze here annually, but that number represents only a fraction of the animals that flooded the meadows at the turn of the century. Biologists say the early, large-scale grazing muddied some streams and eroded hillsides. The national forest has reduced the cattle and sheep allotments to provide better habitat protection for fish, eagles, and big game species. Consistent with its preservation of rivers, the Bridger-Teton is also actively preserving fish and streamside habitat.

From ancient glaciers, underground springs, and winter snows, the upper headwaters of the Snake,

The stark walls of the Breccia Cliffs mark the southern boundary of the Teton Wilderness. The breathtaking rock formation can be viewed from Togwotee Pass. JEFF VANUGA

Green, Yellowstone, and Platte rivers are born in the Bridger-Teton backcountry. These drainages, and others such as the Sweetwater, Bear, and North Platte rivers, support irrigation, hydroelectric power, and municipal water use in a half dozen surrounding states. Each year, the Bridger-Teton exports five million acre feet of water worth an estimated $70 million to users hundreds of miles downstream.

The national forest's rivers and lakes also provide refuge for one of its most famous residents — the trout. With 3,100 miles of streams and 1,200 lakes, the Bridger-Teton is a paradise filled with native and introduced trout species. For fifty miles, the Snake River rolls beneath the Teton Range and rushes through the rugged canyon country south of Jackson. Hidden among the rapids is the Snake River cutthroat trout, the foundation of a fishing industry worth $12 million annually.

Many visitors, however, prefer more isolated areas and can find good fishing in even the remotest spots. During the 1920s and 1930s, naturalists carried rare golden trout to the Wind River Range in milk cans and

A warm glow from an igloo snow cave, right, illuminates nightfall on the Bridger-Teton National Forest. The national forest offers opportunities for recreationists year-round. TOM BEAN

A pair of North American river otters, below, nuzzle in an icy stream. More than seventy species of mammals inhabit the Bridger-Teton, a rich enclave of biological diversity. W. PERRY CONWAY

released them into many of the lakes that today are part of the Bridger Wilderness. Those lakes also hold arctic grayling and brook, rainbow, brown, cutthroat, and lake trout. Each year, flyfishermen and spincasters rack up 100,000 angler days, the third-highest total among the national forests in Greater Yellowstone.

Kayakers and rafters also enjoy the waters of the national forest, particularly the swirling rapids of the Snake River. Two of the Snake's tributaries — the Hoback River and Granite Creek — are considered recreation rivers and make for excellent floating trips.

Motorists can travel the Bridger-Teton along one major artery and a series of secondary roads. U.S. Highway 89 runs north from Alpine Junction, Wyoming, on the west side of the national forest to meet up with U.S. Highway 189/191, which runs north from Pinedale, Wyoming, on the forest's southeastern reaches. The highway continues north through Jackson and on toward the south entrance of Yellowstone National Park.

A colorful spread of sunflowers lights up the base of Togwotee Pass, east of Grand Teton National Park on the Bridger-Teton National Forest.
JEFF VANUGA

Wyoming also has created a scenic Centennial Byway, in honor of the state's 100th birthday in 1990. The route, extending from Dubois to Pinedale, can be completed in one day and illustrates the different faces of the national forest. Starting in Dubois, the byway follows U.S. Highway 287/26 over the dazzling Togwotee Pass to the town of Moran. From there, the route follows U.S. 189/191 south through the heart of Jackson Hole and into the winding Hoback River Canyon to Pinedale.

The national forest contains four other exceptional drives:

• The Gros Ventre Road, dubbed "the gateway to the Gros Ventre Wilderness," is paved from U.S. Highway 89 east to the town of Kelly. East of Kelly, the Gros Ventre Slide Geological Area commemorates a 1925 landslide in which a mountain face splintered and plunged into the Gros Ventre River, damming the river to create Lower Slide Lake. Now a popular destination for wind surfers and fishermen, Lower Slide Lake is a twinkling body of water dotted with old tree snags and large boulders. Four campgrounds in the area serve as excellent places to begin hikes into the surrounding terrain, which is rich in color from mineral deposits. The hills around Lower Slide Lake are among the best sites in the western interior of North America for collecting fossils from the Jurassic Period, when Jackson Hole was covered by a great sea.

• Greys River Road, a gravel route, meanders along the Greys River in the western portion of the national forest through a quiet valley from the Palisades/Alpine area toward the town of LaBarge. Hikes from the road are rewarding, and many people hunt, fish, and camp in this peaceful setting.

Backpackers trek along a well-worn trail in the highlands surrounding Mount Leidy, located in the northern portion of the Bridger-Teton. With Yellowstone National Park to the north and Grand Teton National Park to the west, the Mount Leidy area contains important habitat for big game animals. GEORGE WEURTHNER

Skiing on parts of the Bridger-Teton is almost as close as your front door. Here, the town of Jackson lies at the base of the Snow King Ski Area, located just six blocks from the Jackson Town Square. FRANK S. BALTHIS

• Skyline Drive, a paved road heading east from Pinedale, climbs slowly to the stunning mountains around Fremont Lake, a high alpine lake covering 5,000 surface acres of water. With a depth of 607 feet, Fremont Lake is the seventh deepest natural lake in the lower forty-eight states, excluding the Great Lakes. Located on its northwestern shores is the Redick-Chambers Lodge, a national historic landmark. Set on four acres, the structures were build in the 1920s and operate under a special use permit by the Chambers Historic Trust.

• The Green River Road, a gravel route also known as Forest Road 091, takes visitors to Green River Lakes. Here are a campground, wilderness trailhead, and historic homestead cabins. The area can be reached by taking U.S. Highway 191 and then Wyoming Highway 352 north from Pinedale to the campground. The 11,695-foot summit of Squaretop Mountain rises dramatically beyond the lakes.

Each year, thousands of visitors also drive to the top of 8,431-foot Teton Pass, along the major route between Jackson Hole, Wyoming, and Teton Valley, Idaho. This lofty pass offers panoramic views of the Teton Range and the two bordering states, leaving a lasting impression of the natural beauty that has charmed travelers to this area for centuries.

During the 1980s, the Bridger-Teton began drafting a working plan that will carry national forest managers well into the twenty-first century. If the number of citizens concerned about the forest's future is any indication of its popularity, then it may indeed be one of the most treasured tracts of wild land in the country. Some 20,000 people sent in comments, including residents from several foreign countries and from every state in the nation except Rhode Island.

This intense interest illustrates that even though the Bridger-Teton National Forest lies in the shadow of two national parks, its own features elicit praise and lasting affection from those who visit. ∎

BRIDGER-TETON
NATIONAL FOREST DIRECTORY
GREATER YELLOWSTONE AREA

POINTS OF INTEREST

JACKSON is the administrative headquarters for the national forest and gateway to Grand Teton National Park. The town square contains elk antler archways, while the town has a Wild West flavor.

GANNETT PEAK, the highest point in Wyoming and the Greater Yellowstone area, towers in the Wind River Range at 13,804 feet.

GROS VENTRE SLIDE GEOLOGICAL AREA east of Kelly commemorates a 1925 landslide that plugged the Gros Ventre River to form Lower Slide Lake.

NATIONAL ELK REFUGE, adjacent to the town of Jackson, attracts 9,400 elk fed by wildlife officials each winter. Sleigh rides are available.

WILDERNESS AREAS

TETON 585,468 acres in the northern portion of the national forest near Yellowstone National Park.

GROS VENTRE 287,000 acres west of Jackson.

BRIDGER 428,169 acres on the western face of the Wind River Range that hold some 1,200 alpine lakes.

RECREATIONAL OPPORTUNITIES

HIKING AND RIDING More than 3,000 miles of trail open to hiking and horseback riding, including 220 miles of the Continental Divide National Scenic Trail and the Sheridan National Recreation Trail. The Teton Crest and Phillips Ridge trails along the Teton Range offer panoramic views of Jackson Hole on the east and the Targhee National Forest of Idaho on the west. The Mosquito Creek Trail, south of the Tetons, takes hikers to Mosquito Pass.

CAMPING Nearly four dozen major developed sites and hundreds of opportunities for backcountry use.

SCENIC DRIVES The Wyoming Centennial Scenic Byway, honoring the state's 100th birthday in 1990, extends from Dubois to Pinedale and crosses through the Hoback River Canyon.

KAYAKING AND RAFTING Numerous opportunities for kayaking on the Snake and Hoback rivers. Scenic and whitewater floats available on the Snake River. Commercial operators in Jackson offer trips on the Snake on the hour every summer.

HUNTING Elk, deer, moose, bighorn sheep, and other species. Licenses required from the Wyoming Game and Fish Department.

FISHING Numerous opportunities in the Snake River and mountain lakes throughout the national forest. Check with local wildlife officials for special regulations on catch and release or slot limits. License required.

ALPINE SKIING Jackson Hole at Teton Village (one aerial tram and nine chairlifts), northwest of Jackson, and Snow King (two chairlifts), just south of Jackson.

CROSS-COUNTRY SKIING Available at several local resorts as well as backcountry locations. Teton and Togwotee passes offer numerous opportunities.

SNOWMOBILING The Continental Divide Snowmobile Trail runs from Lander, Wyoming, to the south entrance of Yellowstone National Park and links with other trail systems in eastern Idaho and southern Montana. Dozens of miles of snowmobile trails available elsewhere in the national forest.

OFF-ROAD VEHICLES Trail bikes allowed on side trails and secondary roads, but check with national forest officials for information on any closures. Motorized transportation and mountain bikes are prohibited in wilderness areas.

ADMINISTRATIVE OFFICES

FOREST HEADQUARTERS 340 North Cache, Box 1888, Jackson, WY 83001, (307) 733-2752

JACKSON RANGER DISTRICT Box 1689, Jackson, WY 83001, (307) 733-4755

KEMMERER RANGER DISTRICT Box 31, Kemmerer, WY 83101, (307) 877-4415

BIG PINEY RANGER DISTRICT Box 218, Big Piney, WY 83113, (307) 276-3375

GREYS RIVER RANGER DISTRICT Box 338, Afton, WY 83110, (307) 886-3166

BUFFALO RANGER DISTRICT Box 278, Moran, WY 83013, (307) 543-2386

PINEDALE RANGER DISTRICT Box 220, Pinedale, WY 82941, (307) 367-4326

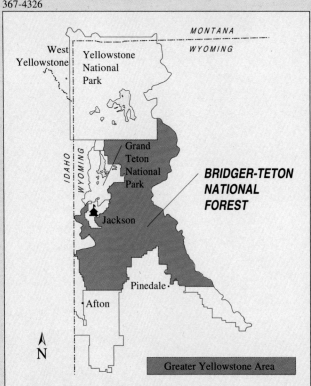

*As maples and aspen don their autumn attire, fall brings a brilliant splash of color to a region
dominated by evergreens. Deciduous trees along the Snake River in the Targhee National Forest
provide important habitat to more than 250 species of wildlife.* HOWARD PHOTOGRAPHY

Targhee

A land of many uses

In 1868 near the frontier outpost of Fort Bridger, an Indian chief named Targhee signed a treaty with the U.S. government, bringing peace to the wooded mountains of eastern Idaho and western Wyoming.

Targhee's pact was viewed as a gesture of friendship between his Bannock tribe and the white settlers who were rapidly moving into the region. The aging chief said nature's beauty is not owned by individuals but shared by all people as part of the public trust. Human respect for wildlife, virgin forests, and streams, Targhee said, would produce a fruitful bounty for all inhabitants.

Those words were a powerful prophecy.

Forty years after the Fort Bridger treaty was signed, Congress declared the Bannock homeland a national forest and gave it the name of its famous leader. Today, road signs in the Targhee National Forest proclaim what the Indians knew all along, that this is "a land of many uses."

The Targhee offers a dramatic milieu that marks the western edge of the Greater Yellowstone area, with all but 400,000 of its 1.8 million acres included in the region. Hemmed between the finest potato cropland in Idaho and the western boundaries of Yellowstone and Grand Teton national parks, these forest lands provide a vital ecological corridor for plants and wildlife.

Five mountain ranges — the Beaverhead, Big Hole,

Neely Cove in the Palisades Roadless Area appears to glow with red snow. The hue actually comes from red algae in the snow. This phenomenon occurs throughout the higher elevations of the Greater Yellowstone area. RALPH MAUGHAN

Centennial, Palisades, and Teton — rise like citadels above sweeping valleys and camel-humped foothills. Lush stands of lodgepole pine, Engelmann spruce, and Douglas-fir cover nearly 80 percent of the Targhee. Since the 1960s, these trees have provided the foundation of a booming logging industry that is a major economic force in the region. While the Targhee's primary export is timber, the national forest also notches 1.3 million recreation visitor days annually.

Because of the national forest's dual mission, resource managers have worked to balance the benefits of tourism, recreation, and hunting with those derived from harvesting raw materials. This philosophy grew out of the Forest Reserve concept pioneered by such early conservationists as Theodore Roosevelt and Gifford Pinchot, the founding father of the national forest system, who believed the public lands should be used wisely for a number of purposes.

Woven together by a fabric of hiking trails, world-class fishing streams, and scenic drives, the Targhee has long been known as a backpacker's national forest. Its trail system spans 1,100 miles of diverse terrain and connects with a network of paved and dirt roads that exceeds 1,350 miles.

When winter wraps a glistening blanket of snow around the Targhee, these same breathtaking routes bustle with a different kind of activity. Snowmobilers and cross-country skiers can take advantage of 580 miles of groomed and semi-groomed trails. The Targhee also serves as a gateway to the snow-covered wonderland of Yellowstone National Park.

At first glance, it might seem as if the adjacent Yellowstone and Grand Teton national parks hold the finest conditions for hiking and camping in the region. After all, the parks are known for their rustic backcountry. But pristine pockets of nature are also found in national forest wilderness areas. And the Targhee contains two brilliant examples of wilderness, just inside the Wyoming state line.

Tucked along the western slope of the Tetons, the 123,451-acre Jedediah Smith Wilderness is a visual feast of snow-laden peaks and dancing streams. The 10,750-acre Winegar Hole Wilderness, pressed against the moody southwestern corner of Yellowstone Park, is a land where grizzlies roam. Together, the wilderness areas make up an ecological gemstone within the Rocky Mountain chain, containing primitive conditions untrammeled by man.

Marked by pitched slopes and craggy peaks that stretch into the clouds, the Continental Divide wriggles through the Targhee. Water, ice, wind, earthquakes, and fire have sculpted a landscape that continues to undergo a natural metamorphosis. The consequences of these phenomena can seem fairly subtle over a short period of time, but occasionally nature unleashes a violent fury of change with lasting effects.

Following a century of fire suppression, the North Fork forest fire of 1988 began in the Targhee and swept into Yellowstone Park to become one of the largest blazes in that year's historic fire season. Near the town of West Yellowstone, Montana, blackened pine snags remind visitors of the fire's rage. But that fire also will lead to a glorious rebirth of the forest canopy in the coming decades. And it pales in comparison to other events that have rocked the Targhee.

Perhaps two million years ago, a volcano on the eastern front of the national forest suddenly erupted, spewing molten lava, boulders, and soot high into the atmosphere. Ashen debris was scattered into regions thousands of miles away, and the crater left behind was several miles long. Today, the crater — known as the Island Park Caldera — is a lush haven for several rare and federally protected species, including grizzlies, trumpeter swans, bald eagles, and peregrine falcons.

The crater also serves as a reminder of the earth's volatility in this western region of Greater Yellowstone. The Targhee's neighbor, Yellowstone Park, sits on top of the most active geologic hot spot on the planet. Flowing just miles beneath the ground, rivers of magma heat underground springs that eventually surface throughout eastern portions of the Targhee. Geologists say mammoth-sized volcanic activity occurs in the region every 600,000 years.

Visitors can survey the heart of the crater bowl by hiking or driving to the Bishop Mountain Lookout, accessible off U.S. Highway 20. Built in 1936 as a tool for spotting forest fires, the

The sight and sound of trumpeter swans in flight are common near the misty waters of Harriman State Park, in the heart of the Targhee National Forest. Surrounded by mountains, these waters host several hundred trumpeter swans during the winter months.
HOWARD PHOTOGRAPHY

Standing like sentinels guarding a priceless treasure, the mountains of the Snake River Range give hikers a bird's eye vantage on the Targhee. The range contains a type of volcanic rock known as rhyolite. HOWARD PHOTOGRAPHY

---

lookout rises 7,810 feet above sea level.

In the West, water is often at a premium. But the Targhee has an abundant supply, drawn from melting snows, tepid springs, and bubbling brooks. The national forest cradles 212 miles of Class One streams, more than any other forest land in the northern Rockies. That classification is reserved for clean rivers with exceptional fisheries.

Water on the Targhee forms important natural highways for wildlife and quenches the thirst of vegetation. Some fifty-two species of mammals and 200 species of birds have found a home on the Targhee. Remarkably, every large mammal species identified in Greater Yellowstone is found on the national forest. In the

heart of the Targhee rises Lionhead Mountain, a rocky summit under consideration for wilderness status. As the aspen explode every autumn in hues of red, yellow, and orange, elk hunters often stalk the animals beneath this peak in hopes of taking a prized rack.

Each winter as deep snows push thousands of elk out of the higher elevations of Yellowstone National Park, many of the animals migrate into the Targhee. Because much of the lower grasslands outside the national park are privately owned and have been developed, river bottoms on the national forest are vital to elk survival during the harsh winters. Elk and deer are often seen grazing west of Ashton and St. Anthony, Idaho, on the Targhee and on private ranches whose owners have agreed to allow wildlife grazing in their pastures.

The grizzly bear also inhabits the Targhee, which with the Gallatin, Shoshone, and Bridger-Teton national forests is considered critical to the future of the massive bear. Biologists say grizzlies are most com-

REDISCOVER A LONG-LOST TREASURE

Years ago, the Mesa Falls Highway near Ashton on Idaho Highway 47 was the main thoroughfare for visitors traveling to the west entrance of Yellowstone National Park. But during the late 1950s, U.S. Highway 20 through Island Park was constructed as an alternative route, and the enchanting drive along the Henrys Fork of the Snake River appeared forgotten forever.

But this long-lost treasure has been rediscovered and turned into the Mesa Falls National Forest Scenic Byway. The route traverses eighteen miles of the Targhee National Forest in Idaho's Fremont County.

This two-lane road offers a memorable detour from U.S. Highway 20. After leaving Ashton, the byway offers spectacular views of the western slope of the Teton Range and drops into a canyon formed by the confluence of the Henrys Fork, Warm River, and Robinson Creek. Later, the road rides near the rim of the Island Park Caldera, one of the largest volcanic craters in the world, and then winds along the Henrys Fork via Warm River Gorge and Bear Gulch.

At Mesa Falls, visitors can take in panoramic views of both the Upper Falls, which plunges 100 feet, and the Lower Falls, crashing seventy feet. Near Upper Mesa Falls stands an old tourist lodge that may someday be converted into a visitor center.

The last stretch of the byway offers a lesson in the way the Forest Service manages natural resources under a "multiple use" philosophy. As the road nears Osborne Meadows and the intersection of U.S. 20, visitors pass through elk migration routes, livestock grazing areas, and stands of trees that might someday be logged for wood products.

Finally, there is Harriman State Park, a lush wildland that provides important habitat for trumpeter swans, bald eagles, elk, and moose. The backcountry trail system in Harriman links to other trails in the Targhee, giving visitors a number of options for day hikes.

The Targhee National Forest and the state of Idaho have jointly promoted the picturesque Mesa Falls area, providing another example of how different government agencies in the Greater Yellowstone area work together to emphasize the recreational assets of public lands.

A rainbow shimmers off the spray from Upper Mesa Falls. Thundering into its 100-foot cascade, the falls provides a scenic stop along Idaho Highway 47, which has been designated the Mesa Falls National Forest Scenic Byway.
GLENN VAN NIMWEGEN

mon near moist river bottoms that hold plenty of fish and vegetation to feed the animal's voracious appetite.

Wandering gently through the floor of the Island Park Caldera is the Henrys Fork of the Snake River, a trout stream of international acclaim. As grizzlies began to recolonize areas outside of Yellowstone Park in recent years, the Henrys Fork has provided important bear habitat. The tranquil river is fed by releases of water from the Island Park Reservoir and gathers momentum from four tributaries — the Buffalo, Warm, and Falls rivers and Robinson Creek.

The majority of the Targhee's 200,000 angler days are recorded on the Henrys Fork and its sister stream, the South Fork of the Snake, which join together east of Idaho Falls. Rippling with cutthroat, brown, brook, and rainbow trout, they are the most heavily used rivers in the national forests of Greater Yellowstone. Both watersheds also support irrigation of potato cropland and drive hydroelectric power downstream.

As the Henrys Fork begins its march toward the Columbia River, its headwaters brush the bucolic setting of Harriman State Park, where hundreds of rare trumpeter swans congregate in open water. The magnificent trumpeters, which average twenty pounds and display a wingspan of up to eight feet, are the largest waterfowl species in the world.

Earlier this century, the trumpeter was headed toward extinction. Two centuries of commercial hunting, combined with loss of habitat, had caused the trumpeter to virtually disappear from the forty-eight contiguous states, where its range had once extended from coast to coast. In the summer of 1932, just sixty-nine of the birds were counted nationwide, all in Yellowstone Park and remote

The relatively high precipitation levels on the Targhee nourish a myriad of plants and wildflowers, such as the Jones columbine, top right. This plant, also known as the limestone columbine, is common on the limestone mountain slopes that flank the Targhee. KRISTI DUBOIS

A bull elk strikes a regal pose, right. The national forest provides crucial winter habitat for elk that leave the confines of Yellowstone National Park for lower ground and available forage. KEN ARCHER

Tucked between a narrow band of mountains on the Wyoming border and the high sagebrush plains of southeastern Idaho, a portion of the Caribou National Forest contributes important habitat for migratory wildlife and native fish in the Greater Yellowstone area. Just 300,000 of the Caribou's 1.2 million acres lie within the ecosystem, and the Caribou's Greater Yellowstone area is administered by Targhee National Forest.

The Caribou area illustrates the importance of water in shaping habitat for plants and animals. During the summer months, when the interior valleys and canyons turn tawny in color, some parts of the landscape appear deceivingly dry in the lower elevations. But it is only an illusion. Crisscrossed by hundreds of creeks and springs, the Caribou actually contains abundant water. Wild animals meander in the fertile watersheds, and wildflowers bloom into a colorful, natural carpet.

The northern tier of the Caribou near Palisades Reservoir is transformed seasonally into one of the richest river-based wildlife sanctuaries in the West, boasting habitat for hundreds of species. The southwest edge of the national forest abuts Grays Lake National Wildlife Refuge, a marshy haven year-round for whooping cranes, sandhill cranes, trumpeter swans, and waterfowl.

Towering between those perpetual oases are camel-humped mountains known as much for their gold deposits as for their majestic vistas. The visual centerpiece is 9,800-foot Caribou Mountain, accentuated by four glacial cirques and shadowing the eastern shores of Grays Lake. Standing beside Caribou Mountain is Bald Mountain, a flat-topped summit that offers panoramic views of the Big Hole, Palisades, and even the Teton ranges in Jackson Hole, Wyoming.

Half of all the streams on the Caribou drain into the Columbia River Basin and feed rivers that run through almost the entire Pacific Northwest. The role of water is especially apparent at the Palisades Reservoir, which marks the intersection of the Caribou, Targhee, and Bridger-Teton national forests.

The immense man-made lake was built to store water for farmers who irrigate eastern Idaho's famous potato belt. Dense stands of pine, spruce, and fir wrap the Palisades Reservoir, which stretches twenty-five miles in length. Dozens of campsites, boat landings, and trails are scattered around the reservoir, which records some 25,000 recreation days annually. While anglers explore the coves in search of trout, windsurfers and water skiers glide across the shimmering waters. In winter, ice fishermen and snowmobilers venture into the area's wind-blown snowscape.

Flowing northwest from the Palisades Dam, the South Fork of the Snake River runs beneath the undulating peaks of the Palisades and Big Hole ranges. Along this quiet corridor of braided side channels and metamorphic cliffs is a trout fishery of international acclaim.

Within the verdant valleys of the Caribou, 250 species of mammals and birds have found a niche, the majority of them in the northern half of the national forest. The Greater Yellowstone portion of the Caribou does not contain any federal wilderness areas. But three unroaded tracts of land currently perform the same function, preserving a feast of primitive conditions in Bear Creek, Caribou, and North Stump Creek.

Nearly every large mammal and raptor species found in the Greater Yellowstone region inhabits the 300,000 acres of the Caribou that fall in Greater Yellowstone, including bighorn sheep, elk, moose, white-tailed and mule deer, foxes, bobcats, and black bears. Although the national forest today is a paradise for wildlife watchers and hunters, the outlook for mule deer, elk, and moose once was bleak. Overhunting in the early 1900s decimated animal populations, leaving fewer than 300 deer and 200 elk. But intensified habitat management has resulted in a steady increase of deer and elk, with populations now numbering in the thousands.

Big game animals benefit from the Caribou's lush stands of aspen and cottonwoods, munching on the broad leaves that explode into blazing hues during the autumn. The Caribou and the Targhee national forests have an exceptional mix of deciduous trees that serve as nesting sites for osprey and, occasionally, bald eagles.

Development of natural resources on the Caribou has focused on gold mining in recent years. While logging and livestock grazing occur on the national forest, new technology has made gold mining more efficient and profitable than in the past.

Hundreds of active mining claims exist on the Caribou, and private companies have targeted places such as Caribou Mountain, which is believed to hold large gold deposits. The Forest Service has sought ways to minimize any disturbance to scenic vistas and has applied regulations designed to ensure the preservation of watersheds.

PART OF GREATER YELLOWSTONE

Mountains frame Palisades Reservoir, a man-made lake that stretches across the Caribou and Targhee national forests. The reservoir is popular with recreationists in both the summer and winter months. HOWARD PHOTOGRAPHY

Phosphate mining has found its way to Soda Springs, an area where travertine terraces rise from the earth and resemble features found hundreds of miles away at Mammoth Hot Springs in Yellowstone National Park. These rare geological formations, however, are smaller and fed by cold — rather than hot — water. Private conservation groups have purchased land in the Formation Springs area to protect the few travertine springs that still remain.

This area also holds poignant remnants of another era. The ground still bears the marks of wagon trains that rolled westward on some of the nation's legendary pioneer trails. At one time, the Oregon Trail skirted the Bear River and passed through the towns of Sage, Montpelier, and Soda Springs. The California Trail wound through the region and into Sublette Canyon, and the Lander Trail connected Wyoming's Star Valley with the Stump Creek drainage.

Some pioneers settled in the region, to prospect for gold. The ghost towns of Keenan City and Caribou City can be reached by taking Forest Service Road 87 between Herman and the Palisades Reservoir.

Motorists can treat themselves to a tour of the pioneer landscape without leaving their cars. Tin Cup Highway (Idaho Highway 34) is one of the loveliest drives on the national forest. The state of Idaho has designated the 57-mile route between Soda Springs and Freedom, Wyoming, as a pioneer, historic, and scenic byway. It passes through a spectacular canyon and offers opportunities to view moose, elk, and livestock grazing in the sweet grasslands. Another drive begins at Grays Lake and crosses the forest interior to McCoy Creek on the shores of Palisades Reservoir. This eighteen-mile stretch, known as the McCoy Road, offers noble views of Big Elk Mountain about eight miles west of McCoy Creek.

waters around the Targhee.

To save the species, emergency measures were undertaken, and the nearby Red Rock Lakes National Wildlife Refuge was established across the border in Montana as a sanctuary for the rare birds in 1935. Fortunately, the population of migratory and resident trumpeters rebounded. About 1,750 swans today converge for part of the year in wetlands around eastern Idaho, western Wyoming, and southern Montana. The Henrys Fork on the Targhee and Red Rock Lakes harbor most of these elegant creatures.

Three years after Red Rock Lakes was established, an earth-filled dam measuring ninety-one feet in height and 1,250 feet in length was built upstream from Harriman State Park to store water for irrigators. Stream flows on the Henrys Fork are controlled by this dam, which forms Island Park Reservoir. Above the dam, visitors may see flashes of bright red in tributary streams, as kokanee salmon make their spawning run.

The marshlands that connect Henrys Lake with the Island Park Reservoir are part of the Big Springs National Recreation Water Trail, a five-mile stretch of the North Fork of the Snake River that gives floaters a leisurely opportunity to view wildlife. The Centennial

Mountains form a stunning backdrop for this aquatic route, which starts near the Big Springs Campground and ends at Macks Inn. Chief Joseph led his Nez Perce tribe through this region during his historic flight from the U.S. Cavalry. Travelers here may spot Johnny Sack Cabin, a rustic log structure listed in the National Register of Historic Places.

The Targhee, well-known for its recreational opportunities, is also known for its timber production. During the 1960s, the national forest initiated one of the most ambitious logging efforts in the Greater Yellowstone region. To combat pine beetle infestation and salvage logs affected by the stubborn insect, a logging boom began that still continues.

In fact, the Targhee accounts for half of all the timber cut on national forests in the Greater Yellowstone area. Well over one billion board feet of pine, spruce, and fir has been harvested by private companies. Visitors driving along U.S. Highway 20 north of Ashton can see the legacy of this industry. The Targhee features a roadside public education program to show where trees have been cut and where new trees have begun to grow in reforestation efforts.

Approximately 180,000 acres — or 19 percent of the forest lands suitable for logging — lie within terrain deemed critical to the grizzly bear. Thus the Targhee is under pressure to accommodate logging while protecting animals that make the national forest their home. Over the next ten years, the annual timber harvest on the Targhee will drop from an average of 86 million board feet to 35 million board feet to ensure the preservation of key wildlife areas. This modification of the timber program is an example of how the national forest is adapting to calls to expand tourism and enhance wildlife habitat.

Another example is livestock grazing. Roughly 181,000 acres of the Targhee are classified as excellent range for livestock, accounting for well over half the best rangeland in the Greater Yellowstone area.

The Targhee once allowed hundreds of thousands of cattle and sheep to graze

Hikers cross a creek on the Targhee National Forest. Many streams on this national forest boast world-class trout fishing. FRANK S. BALTHIS

upon the rich grass. But national forest rangeland managers soon discovered problems with overgrazing, such as damage to some of the world-class streams. Today, the approximately 21,000 cattle and 87,000 sheep allowed to graze on the Targhee represent merely a fraction of their former herds, and the national forest is a leader in trying to protect water quality in local streams.

By reducing livestock grazing on the national forest, the Targhee has sought to minimize conflicts with grizzly bears and emphasize sport fishing through a nationwide Forest Service program aimed at restoring stream habitat for fish. The Targhee has employed habitat-saving measures such as in-stream structures and the planting of willows in more than 2,600 stream locations.

The Targhee contains more surface acre feet of water than any other national forest in Greater Yellowstone, largely because of the voluminous Palisades Reservoir above the South Fork River. Hiking trails and roads extend from the reservoir, bringing visitors within a stone's throw of waterfalls, travertine springs, and the Snake River Mountains (also known as the Palisades Range). The Palisades Reservoir — with its eight boat ramps and dozens of campsites — is a popular destination for boaters, anglers, and water-skiers during the summer months.

Visitors who want challenging terrain away from developed areas usually turn to the Ashton, Teton Basin, and Palisades ranger districts in the southern half of the Targhee. Few mountain ranges in the country can rival the noble

---

A mammalian chameleon, the snowshoe hare, top right, often escapes notice because its fur changes color along with the seasons. In summer, its coat is brown. In winter, it's white. The snowshoe hare, common in the national forest, is an important source of food for lynx, mountain lions, and owls. TOM MURPHY

A lone bicyclist, bottom right, travels a quiet road in the Targhee National Forest. Bicycling is just one of the many ways to enjoy the peaceful settings of the national forests.
GLENN OAKLEY

A SANCTUARY FOR WILDLIFE

Carving a serpentine path through the arid sagebrush plains of eastern Idaho, the Snake River provides an oasis of sorts for wildlife. A formidable source of water that flows through three states, the Snake starts on the Bridger-Teton National Forest in Wyoming and empties 1,056 miles later into the mighty Columbia River in western Washington state. In between, it shapes the geography, ecology, and culture of the landscape.

The South Fork of the Snake dramatically illustrates this point as it crosses both the Caribou and Targhee national forests before leaving the Greater Yellowstone area northeast of Idaho Falls.

Rated as one of the finest trout fisheries in the world, the South Fork meanders for fifty-one miles through the Big Hole Mountains and across cropland that produces Idaho's famed potatoes. Driving along U.S. Highway 26, visitors will discover how important the South Fork is to local and migratory wildlife populations. This blue-ribbon stream supports more than fifty species of mammals and 180 species of birds along its banks. With the exception of grizzly bears and bighorn sheep, all the mammals of the Greater Yellowstone area are present here.

Wildlife officials say the South Fork is one of the true ecological gems outside of Yellowstone National Park and in the entire Pacific Northwest, unsurpassed in terms of river-based wildlife habitat. Twelve breeding pairs of bald eagles nest on the South Fork during the summer, and another eighty of the federally protected raptors arrive during the winter. The river also provides habitat for peregrine falcons,

A mature bald eagle keeps an eye out for fish, one of its primary sources of food. The head feathers of these eagles turn white as they age, so young eagles do not wear the distinctive markings. TIM CHRISTIE

osprey, trumpeter swans, whooping cranes, and great blue herons.

But the river is renowned for its fishery, which also is an important indicator for measuring the health of all species. During a recent fish census, biologists with the Idaho Department of Fish and Game estimated the cutthroat trout population at 3,500 per mile and the whitefish population at 30,000 per mile. The riffle-filled waters of the South Fork also have produced the unofficial state record for brown trout at 32 lbs., 2 ozs. Such extraordinary numbers explain the popularity of this river, which annually records 120,000 visitor recreation days.

Roughly thirty miles of the South Fork abut the Caribou National Forest. But its management falls to the Palisades District of the Targhee

National Forest, which also administers the 6,400-acre Snake River Management Area. The Targhee is working now with other state and federal agencies to draft a river management plan to ensure better protection of the South Fork's water quality. Development activity — including grazing, timber production, and motorized recreation — is closely monitored to measure the effects on resident and migratory wildlife populations. Recreation use in both the Caribou and Targhee national forests focuses on hunting, fishing, scenic floating, motor boating, trail bike and horseback riding, kayaking, rock climbing, and hiking.

Those interested in exploring the South Fork can obtain information on fishing restrictions and river use from the Idaho Department of Fish and Game.

profile of the Tetons. Tumbling toward the rolling plains of Teton Valley, this jagged ensemble of peaks marked a point of rendezvous for fur trappers nearly two centuries ago. Possibly as early as 1819, French trappers looked to the summits and proclaimed them Les Trois Tetons, or "the three breasts." Historians say English-speaking mountain men called them Pilot Knobs. However, the French name stuck.

The Jedediah Smith Wilderness, named after one of the original mountain men, is nestled within the bosom of the Teton range. From the Idaho communities of Tetonia, Victor, and Driggs, the west-facing ridgeline can be reached from the famed Alaska Basin and Teton Crest trails. Ascending and wiggling their way through tundra-like meadows, the trails afford unsurpassed panoramic views of Idaho and Wyoming. The western approach — penetrating the most remote contours of the Tetons — even caught the discriminating eyes of famed frontier photographer William Henry Jackson.

Far below in the Teton Valley, Idaho Highway 32 between Ashton and Tetonia provides a scenic prelude to the precipitously steep climb over Teton Pass. Connecting Victor, Idaho, with Wilson, Wyoming, twelve miles away, the highway dissects a rumpled belt of mountains once stumped by John Colter, who trapped beaver in the local creeks. Teton Pass itself attracts telemark and cross-country skiers as soon as the first snow flies. Generally accessible year-round, the highway has been known to close temporarily in the winter due to avalanches.

Snow on the western slopes of the Tetons and throughout the national forest is measured in feet, rather than inches. The winter season transforms the Targhee into a nordic and alpine heaven.

The Grand Targhee Ski Area, hugging the base of Peaked and Freds mountains east of Driggs, is legendary for its waist-deep powder and rewards the downhill skier who wants a broad range of intermediate and expert runs. Skiers are carried to the 10,250-foot summit, which offers astounding views of Grand Teton Mountain. The resort has sixty-two runs and 2,250 vertical feet of terrain. Grand Targhee's snow depth, which reaches up to 500 inches annually, ranks among the highest of all ski areas in the West.

The Kelly Canyon Ski Area east of Idaho Falls on U.S. Highway 26 is much smaller, but popular among local residents during the weekends. For the hardy winter adventurer, Teton Pass remains a bargain for snowboarders and telemark and backcountry skiers who want solitude and untracked slopes. Cross-country enthusiasts can turn to practically any drainage in the Targhee's five mountain ranges for flat and steep

A pilgrim of the marsh, the red-winged blackbird, above, is among the more than 220 species of birds found on the Targhee. Named for the fiery color on its wing, it flourishes along the Henrys Fork of the Snake River. MICHAEL S. SAMPLE

trails. The national forest provides information on all backcountry use, and visitors should check with local ranger districts for current avalanche conditions.

The Targhee also is a mecca for snowmobilers, and with good reason. The national forest lies on the edge of a major snowmobiling hub. The town of West Yellowstone, Montana, bills itself as as "the snowmobile capital of the world." Each winter, nearly 250,000 snowmobilers use the town as a base camp for exploring the groomed trails of Yellowstone Park and the wooded terrain of the Targhee and Gallatin national forests.

Among the premier snowmobile areas in the country is the Two Top National Snowmobile Recreation Trail, which attracts 80,000 snowmobilers annually. Located ten miles west of West Yellowstone, the trail leads to the upper headwalls of 8,710-foot Two Top Mountain. Snowmobilers have access to 200 miles of groomed trail and several warming huts on the Targhee and Gallatin, as well as another 300 miles of trail around West Yellowstone and Fremont County, Idaho.

With all of its winter activity, the national forest shines as a four-season playground. It also has served as a bellwether for gauging development that is compatible with its rich scenic heritage.

If Chief Targhee were to visit his homeland, he might marvel at the many uses being made of it. The Targhee remains a special place with rich rewards — just as the Bannock leader intended. ∎

The stone face of the Snake River Mountains peeks out from behind fall foliage. The mountains, also known as the Palisades, tower near the popular Palisades Reservoir area. HOWARD PHOTOGRAPHY

TARGHEE
NATIONAL FOREST DIRECTORY
GREATER YELLOWSTONE AREA

POINTS OF INTEREST

ISLAND PARK CALDERA is one of the largest volcanic craters in the world. The volcano's eruption 600,000 years ago unleashed a fury 5,000 times greater than the 1980 eruption of Mount St. Helens in Washington state.

HENRYS FORK OF THE SNAKE RIVER at Harriman State Park, along U.S. Highway 20, boasts the largest gathering of trumpeter swans during the winter months and was key in bringing trumpeters back from the brink of extinction.

WILDERNESS AREAS

JEDEDIAH SMITH 123,451 acres along the rim of the Teton Range.

WINEGAR HOLE 10,750 acres near the southwest corner of Yellowstone National Park.

RECREATIONAL OPPORTUNITIES

HIKING AND RIDING More than 1,100 miles of hiking and horseback trail crisscross the national forest. Check with the local ranger district office for any restrictions on horse travel. The Continental Divide National Scenic Trail touches part of the Targhee south of Red Rock Lakes National Wildlife Refuge. The Alaska Basin and Teton Crest trails skirt the crest of the Teton Range.

CAMPING Nearly three dozen developed sites across the national forest. Hundreds of excellent sites available in wilderness and other remote regions of the national forest.

SCENIC DRIVES The Mesa Falls National Forest Scenic Byway on Idaho Highway 47 north of Ashton is an enchanting drive along the Henrys Fork of the Snake River that takes visitors to upper and lower Mesa Falls. Idaho Highway 33 between Victor and Ashton passes through scenic farm country and offers good views of the Teton Range.

KAYAKING AND RAFTING The Henrys and South forks of the Snake River offer opportunities for scenic rafting and kayaking. The Palisades and Island Park reservoirs and the South Fork have boat launch ramps. The Big Springs National Recreation Water Trail on the Island Park Ranger District provides excellent opportunities for viewing wildlife via canoe.

HUNTING Trophy moose, mule deer, and elk, along with good waterfowl and game bird hunting. Licenses required from the Idaho Department of Fish and Game.

FISHING World-class trout fishing on the Henrys and South forks of the Snake River. Good angling on the Teton River and other small streams, as well. Check for regulations on catch and release or slot limits. Licenses required.

ALPINE SKIING Grand Targhee Ski Area east of Driggs and Kelly Canyon Ski Area on U.S. Highway 26.

CROSS-COUNTRY SKIING Thirty-one miles of groomed trails and hundreds of miles of ungroomed trail available, especially for backcountry and telemark skiers and snowboarders in the vicinity of Teton Pass.

SNOWMOBILING Immediate access to more than 580 miles of groomed trail. One of the finest snowmobile trails in the region, the Two Top National Recreation Trail, crosses both the Targhee and Gallatin national forests before climbing to the summit of Two Top Mountain.

OFF-ROAD VEHICLES Trail bike riding is allowed on many trails and secondary dirt roads. Check with local ranger districts for more information.

ADMINISTRATIVE OFFICES

FOREST HEADQUARTERS P.O. Box 208, St. Anthony, ID 83445, (208) 624-3151

ASHTON RANGER DISTRICT P.O. Box 858, Ashton, ID 83420, (208) 652-7442

PALISADES RANGER DISTRICT 3659 East Ririe Highway, Idaho Falls, ID 83401, (208) 523-1412

TETON BASIN RANGER DISTRICT P.O. Box 127, Driggs, ID 83422, (208) 354-2431

ISLAND PARK RANGER DISTRICT P.O. Box 220, Island Park, ID 83429, (208) 558-7301

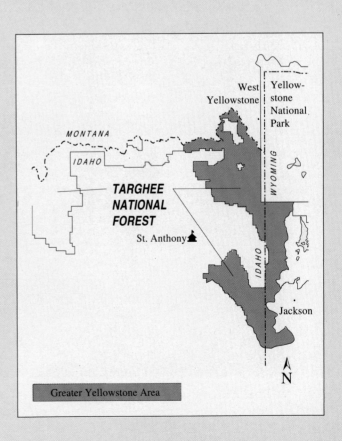

Greater Yellowstone Area

The Lima Peaks edge the meadows of the Little Sheep Creek drainage, near Lima, Montana. The drainage is a popular recreation area, offering good fishing, hunting, and backpacking opportunities. GEORGE WUERTHNER

Beaverhead

Where a frontier atmosphere remains

It is difficult to imagine a public wildland with more scenic charm than the Beaverhead National Forest in southwest Montana, where the broad, azure horizons provide a canopy for a brilliant natural tapestry of rivers, woods, and mountains.

Framed by the pastoral wetlands of the Centennial Valley to the south, the Madison Range to the east, the Pintler Range and Tobacco Root Mountains to the north, and the Bitterroot Mountains to the west, the Beaverhead offers a bonanza of diverse plants and wildlife.

Over the centuries, a half dozen Indian nations claimed the Beaverhead as tribal homelands, following great herds of bison, elk, and deer. Later, French fur trappers traveled the alpine watersheds to gather beaver pelts. At the dawn of the nineteenth century, explorers Lewis and Clark noted the Beaverhead's attributes in amorous detail, writing of crashing waterfalls and effervescent streams.

By the 1860s, miners combed the hillsides hoping to find gold. They left behind a legacy of ghost towns, some of which still remain. On the open range, ranchers flooded the forest highlands with cattle and sheep that grazed the lush grasses there. And logging companies, impressed by glorious stands of spruce, pine, and fir, transformed trees into wood for homes and ties for the expanding railroad.

All of these activities occurred years before the lands

Buttressed by ribs of metamorphic rock, Black Butte climbs above the nearby Madison Valley and offers views of the Snowcrest Range to the west. This angular crest is a prominent fixture in the Gravelly Range. TIM EGAN

that now make up the Beaverhead were set aside in the early 1900s. About one-sixth of this national forest's 2.4 million acres falls within the northeast corner of Greater Yellowstone.

Set among the saw-toothed rims of the Madison, Gravelly, Snowcrest, Tobacco Root, and Centennial mountain ranges, the Greater Yellowstone portion of the Beaverhead has been shaped by numerous forces.

For example, the Madison Range has weathered a continuous barrage of wind, ice, fire, and earthquakes that sculpted a collection of glorious and lofty peaks. Although the Gravellys, Snowcrests, and Centennials are younger — geologically speaking — than the Madisons, they have their own majesty.

For the hiker, horseback rider, and backcountry skier, the Beaverhead has designed an extensive trail system that connects with a network of developed roadways. While many of the primitive roads were built to support mining and grazing operations, they now provide easy access to campgrounds and isolated

fishing streams. The Continental Divide National Scenic Trail, one of the premier hiking routes in the country, runs along the crest of the Divide from the Anaconda-Pintler Wilderness to the Centennial Valley rim.

Although Yellowstone and Grand Teton national parks lie at the center of the twelve million-acre Greater Yellowstone area, visitors seeking primitive conditions often turn to national forest wilderness for solitude. They can find it on the Beaverhead in the Lee Metcalf Wilderness.

Shared with the Gallatin National Forest, the Lee Metcalf is the only wilderness area in the Beaverhead that lies within Greater Yellowstone. Known for its wildlife and glacier-carved headwalls, the wilderness contains several mountain peaks distinguished by cirque basins, talus chutes, and ice-packed snowfields. These mountaintops also offer views of the Tobacco Root Mountains and Gravelly Range.

If ever a wilderness area were designed to tantalize

the senses, the Lee Metcalf succeeds with the Spanish Peaks in the northeastern flank of the national forest. The word "peaks" truly describes the regal grace of these mountains, for their pointed summits preside over an astounding array of forest lands.

Grizzly bears, a federally protected species, are sometimes seen strolling along the drainages of the Lee Metcalf, particularly in the Spanish Peaks and farther south in the Madison Range. About 200 grizzlies survive in the Greater Yellowstone region today, and the powerful bruins have begun recolonizing pockets of the Beaverhead after sharp declines in their numbers during the early 1970s.

Wildlife biologists have designated 68,000 acres of the Greater Yellowstone portion of the Beaverhead as "Situation II" grizzly habitat, meaning grizzlies inhabit the area but are not common. The rustic Lee Metcalf, however, is viewed as an important biological bridge that allows grizzlies to expand their range by migrating from Yellowstone Park into the Beaverhead. During the late summer and early autumn months, grizzlies leave the high country, but not before gorging themselves on a favorite snack — whitebark pine nuts.

The Beaverhead also holds every native big game species in Greater Yellowstone except the bison. The national forest contains more than fifty-five species of mammals and 200 species of birds. The more rugged environs contain the largest antelope and mountain goat populations in the ecosystem, the second-largest concentration of bighorn sheep, and rapidly growing numbers of moose and white-tailed deer.

These populations have made the Beaverhead a hunter's paradise. But the national forest is also known for its role in preserving habitat for rare, threatened, and endangered species such as grizzlies, bald eagles, and trumpeter swans. Fully 2,000 acres are considered prime habitat for nesting eagles.

Along the Beaverhead's southern border, the Continental Divide passes the Red Rock Lakes National Wildlife Refuge near Lima. A shimmering focal point in the Centennial Valley, Red Rock is the site of a major triumph in wildlife conservation. Here, the trumpeter swan was rescued from the brink of extinction.

A flowing creek in the Pioneer Mountains creates lush growing conditions for riparian plants. Creeks such as these feed the larger rivers that cut through the quiet valleys of the Beaverhead. MICHAEL S. SAMPLE

At one time, trumpeters could be found from coast to coast. But the snowy white birds nearly disappeared after centuries of commercial hunting and loss of habitat. By the early 1930s, only sixty-nine were counted nationwide, all in the remote waterways around Yellowstone Park and in the Centennial Valley.

In 1935, the federal government designated the Red Rock refuge a sanctuary for the imperiled trumpeter. That action paid off, for today about 1,750 swans congregate seasonally at Red Rock and in parts of eastern Idaho and western Wyoming. The trumpeter, which has a wingspan of eight feet and weighs up to twenty pounds, is the largest waterfowl species in the world. Visitors to the Beaverhead Valley may be treated to the sight of trumpeters winging by on their descent toward Red Rock.

A major wildlife issue of the 1990s involves the gray wolf, with proposals under consideration to reintroduce wolves into nearby Yellowstone Park. Wolves, coyotes, bobcats, and mountain lions were hunted in the entire Greater Yellowstone area decades ago by government bounty hunters who were called to stop the predators from killing domestic

A trumpeter swan in the Red Rock Lakes National Wildlife Refuge guards its nest. The trumpeter, once near extinction, is the largest waterfowl species in the world and may be seen in the Beaverhead area.
MICHAEL S. SAMPLE

The Beaverhead National Forest borders the Red Rock Lakes National Wildlife Refuge in the heart of the Centennial Valley, a verdant and marshy area that unfolds before the mountain range of the same name. The wildlife sanctuary was established to protect the rare trumpeter swan and offers refuge to 250 other bird species.
MICHAEL S. SAMPLE

WHAT'S IN A NAME?

Nearly all the national forests in Greater Yellowstone have names steeped in American history. But those of the Beaverhead and Gallatin are perhaps most connected to the westward expansion of the white man.

Both of these national forests played central roles in the adventures of Meriwether Lewis and William Clark, who explored the territory the United States gained from France in the Louisiana Purchase. Lewis and Clark followed the Missouri River from Missouri all the way to its headwaters in Montana, embarking on a mission that took them several years to complete.

Lewis and Clark's famed female guide Sacagawea, a Shoshone Indian, is reponsible for giving the Beaverhead its name. During the summer of 1805, Sacagawea pointed out a rock feature resembling a beaver's head, long used as a landmark by her people. The formation has been preserved as a state monument along Montana Highway 41. And it gave the Beaverhead River and Beaverhead County their names.

The Gallatin National Forest takes its name from Albert Gallatin, who in 1780 left his native Switzerland and emigrated to the American colonies, where he served in the Revolutionary War. He later was elected to both the U. S. House of Representatives and the U. S. Senate. A proven leader, he was appointed secretary of the Treasury by President Thomas Jefferson in 1802.

Gallatin's name, however, was immortalized for his involvement with Lewis and Clark. As Treasury secretary, Gallatin was a key figure in securing financing for the expedition. In return, Lewis and Clark gave his name to one of the three streams — the Gallatin, Madison, and Jefferson — that come together at Three Forks and form the Missouri River. And on February 10, 1899, President William McKinley established the 80,000-acre Gallatin Forest Reserve, which Congress later changed to the Gallatin National Forest.

Sphinx Mountain at sunset offers an enchanting view of the Beaverhead National Forest. The horizon yields first the Snowcrest Mountains and, farther along, the gentle lines of the Pioneer and Tobacco Root mountains. PETE AND ALICE BENGEYFIELD

A backpacker takes in a view of the Taylor-Hilgard Mountains, above, whose serrated ridges have been carved by glaciers, earthquakes, and wind. The Beaverhead makes an epic-sized outdoor classroom for amateur geologists. MICHAEL S. SAMPLE

A black bear cub, left, peeks through the fork of a tree. The bears are prevalent on the Beaverhead. In the spring cubs emerge from the den and are quickly weaned of their mother's milk before adopting a diet consisting primarily of roots and berries. MICHAEL FRANCIS

An elk calf wanders through a green meadow typical of the grasslands found on the Beaverhead. The national forest's lush grasses support both livestock and wildlife. MICHAEL S. SAMPLE

livestock. All but the wolf recovered, and it appears the only way to re-establish a viable population is to return the animals artificially.

If wolves are placed in the national park, biologists predict the population eventually will grow large enough that they will move into adjacent national forests. Because of its abundance of elk and deer — the wolf's primary source of food — the Beaverhead could someday provide habitat for the animals.

Nothing is more important to the survival of wildlife on the national forest than clean water. The moisture-rich slopes of the Beaverhead nourish primarily lodgepole pine, along with Douglas-fir and Engelmann spruce, on about 40 percent of the forest lands. The remainder opens to breathtaking sweeps of wildflowers and grassy knolls. Once the snowpack melts, well over half the higher glens contain cattle and sheep, giving the national forest a frontier flavor reminiscent of the Old West.

Resource development continues on the Beaverhead, but at a slower pace than before.

Livestock grazing has been reduced since the turn of the century, when domestic cattle and sheep numbering in the hundreds of thousands were driven onto the Beaverhead. Because they sometimes concentrate in stream bottoms, they can trample vegetation and weaken stream banks. Any resulting erosion can cause sedimentation problems that affect water quality.

Cattle and sheep also compete with big game animals that rely upon the grasses in lower elevations during the winter months, when weather conditions turn harsh. Some 10,000 cattle, horses, and sheep graze on the Beaverhead annually, and forest managers are working to reduce conflicts between livestock and wildlife habitat. More than 700 structural improvements, including fences, have been made to improve rangelands and keep livestock out of sensitive drainages.

Sagebrush, that enduring symbol of the open range, flourishes at the base of the Centennial Mountains. Within a 4,000-foot vertical stretch, visitors to the Beaverhead can climb from the warmth of spring to snowcapped peaks above treeline. The diverse terrain contains a variety of habitats for wildlife and plants. MICHAEL S. SAMPLE

In recent years, some ten million board feet of timber has been harvested annually. And approximately 5,000 active mining claims exist for gold, copper, silver, talc, gypsum, and other minerals.

Backpackers in the Beaverhead will occasionally stumble upon the remains of gold mines, which were once prolific during the prospecting era of more than a century ago. Ghost towns northwest of the Greater Yellowstone area near Dillon are reminders of the mining boom that brought thousands of settlers into the region seeking their fortune.

Visitors here can enjoy a variety of recreational choices on foot or by car.

The Gravelly Range Road, a scenic loop, unveils the splendors of high mountain country by taking visitors on a dirt road fifty miles long. The route provides plenty of opportunity for viewing the mountain ranges fading east into Yellowstone Park and is a sure bet for wildlife watchers. The road also passes a series of streams that nourish larger rivers far below in the valleys.

The Greater Yellowstone portion of the Beaverhead contains nearly 100 miles of streams, including the Madison River, a world-class fishery that brushes the Beaverhead's eastern tier. U.S. Highway 287 running south of the flyfishing center of Ennis is a gateway to the national forest and the Madison River country.

The Madison Range, named by Lewis and Clark, is known for its high-altitude hiking trails. Here, Echo Peak towers above Expedition Lake and offers a panoramic glimpse of five different mountain ranges.
MICHAEL S. SAMPLE

At the Beaverhead's Madison Ranger District in Ennis, visitors can pick up information on more than 250 lakes and the many campsites sprinkled all across the national forest. Cabins and boat rentals are available at Elk and Wade lakes. Practically every drainage in the Gravellys contains a trailhead for hikers. Fossil hunters should consider a jaunt up Beartrap Canyon to 9,775-foot Specimen Butte and 9,709-foot Monument Mountain, both of which face Fossil Ridge to the east.

Special use permits are required to collect fossils and Indian artifacts.

In many ways, the Beaverhead's blend of wildlife and scenery has produced the quintessential landscape of the American West, where natural forces have influenced the direction of human development. Its mountains inspire and its forests warm the sensitivities of those who visit, making it a welcome environment for all. ■

Sunset casts a glow on the Beaverhead's Centennial Valley, which is rimmed by the Centennial Mountains to the north and the Gravelly Range to the south. MICHAEL S. SAMPLE

BEAVERHEAD
NATIONAL FOREST DIRECTORY
GREATER YELLOWSTONE AREA

POINTS OF INTEREST

RED ROCK LAKES NATIONAL WILDLIFE REFUGE sits outside the southern border of the national forest near Lima, Montana. The federal refuge is home to 258 species of birds, including the rare trumpeter swan.

THE MADISON VALLEY west of the Madison Range and south of Ennis, Montana, teems with elk and antelope migrating to lower elevations during the winter months. The Madison River slices through the valley floor amid colorful cliff walls.

MADISON RIVER CANYON EARTHQUAKE AREA is located just outside the Beaverhead border on the Gallatin National Forest, along U.S. Highway 287 between Ennis and West Yellowstone. The site features information on a 1959 earthquake that killed twenty-eight people.

WILDERNESS AREAS

LEE METCALF About 100,000 acres on the Beaverhead, containing such features as the Spanish Peaks and the Madison Range.

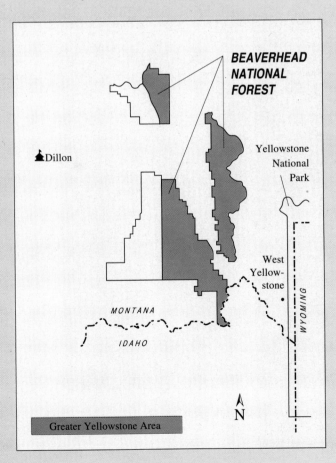

RECREATIONAL OPPORTUNITIES

HIKING AND RIDING More than 300 miles of hiking trails, most of which are also suitable for horseback riding. Check with the Madison Ranger District in Ennis for any special restrictions. The Continental Divide National Scenic Trail intersects part of the Beaverhead north of the Red Rock Lakes National Wildlife Refuge.

CAMPING Eighty campsites in seven developed campgrounds at Ennis, Wade Lake, Cliff Lake, Hilltop, on the Madison River, at West Fork, Jackson Creek, and Potosi. Hundreds of other backcountry campsites also exist.

SCENIC DRIVES The Beaverhead offers a self-guided tour on the Gravelly Loop Road, which runs through cattle country. The Lima Road to Red Rock Lake and U.S. Highway 278 along the Madison River also offer scenic views, while the Standard Creek Road south of Ennis travels through a timber harvest area.

KAYAKING AND RAFTING The Madison River is open to rafting, kayaking, and canoeing. Small boats are permitted on the Ruby River.

HUNTING Elk, deer, and game birds. Licenses required from the Montana Department of Fish, Wildlife, and Parks.

FISHING The Madison River and a dozen alpine lakes offer excellent trout fishing. State licenses required. Check for special regulations relating to catch and release or slot limits.

ALPINE SKIING Maverick Mountain (one chair lift and one pony lift), located thirty-eight miles northwest of Dillon.

CROSS-COUNTRY SKIING Hiking trails are open to cross-country skiing in the winter, but are not groomed.

OFF-ROAD VEHICLES Many dirt roadways and some trails crisscrossing remote sections of the national forest are open to trail bikes. A map showing vehicle travel routes can be purchased at any Beaverhead National Forest office.

ADMINISTRATIVE OFFICES

FOREST HEADQUARTERS 610 North Montana Street, Dillon, MT 59725, (406) 683-3900

MADISON RANGER DISTRICT 5 Forest Service Road, Ennis, MT 59729, (406) 682-4253

Crimson spires in the Spanish Peaks reflect not only the early morning light of alpenglow but also the calming moods of the Gallatin National Forest. Spanish Lake is a popular destination for recreationists. The lake and its namesake mountain range lie within the Lee Metcalf Wilderness Area. TOM FERRIS

Gallatin

The land between the rivers

Little wonder the Gallatin National Forest instills a sense of wonder in those who visit. When the wind blows gently eastward from the Continental Divide, one can imagine the waving pines and sagebrush meadows singing ballads of the frontier West.

In 1806, while the United States was still an infant nation, Meriwether Lewis and William Clark boldly trekked across the heavenly environs of southwestern Montana. Surrounded by majestic peaks and rolling rivers, they discovered why the Indians had viewed this region with spiritual reverence for nearly 10,000 years. Teeming with wildlife, covered with thick stands of lodgepole pine, Englemann spruce, and subalpine fir, and capped by inspiring rock palisades, this was a land of great promise.

The same visual feast remains today for those who visit what is now the Gallatin National Forest, which borders the northwestern edges of Yellowstone National Park. Recording 2.5 million visitor days annually, the Gallatin is the most popular national forest in Montana. Bold mountaintops dominate the skyline here. Six serrated ranges — the Gallatins, Madisons, Beartooths, Bridgers, Absarokas, and Crazies — tower above the sweeping valleys and spacious meadows. Meandering beneath the summits are a trio of pastoral rivers — the Gallatin, Madison, and Yellowstone. A pair of wilderness areas and a smattering of developed recreation areas accentuate the national forest's rich diversity. Stitching together this remarkable natural fabric are more than 2,000 miles of hiking trails and more than 1,000 miles of inventoried roads.

Forty-one percent of this 1.7 million-acre national forest has been set aside in the Absaroka-Beartooth and the Lee Metcalf wilderness areas, which preserve natural ecosystems and nurture primitive conditions that can exceed even the backcountry of national parks.

The Absaroka-Beartooth Wilderness, so named because it flanks the backbone of the Absaroka and Beartooth mountains, is an alpine paradise filled with wildlife. This gargantuan wilderness, covering 930,000 acres, sprawls across two states and portions of the Gallatin, Custer, and Shoshone national forests. Snow-capped summits and active glaciers dominate the tundra environment for seven to eight months of the year, creating a wonderfully Spartan place of earth tones and boulders laced with lichen. But the end of July sees an explosion of wildflowers that form a lustrous backdrop for backcountry visitors.

Below treeline, the wilderness is marked by radiant stands of timber and sleepy mountain brooks. The Absaroka-Beartooth records the highest use of any wilderness in Montana, drawing a loyal contingent of backpackers, climbers, hunters, and anglers. Follow any drainage on the eastern rim of Paradise Valley to soak in the splendor of wilderness. Pine Creek Campground, located off the East River Road on the edge of the wilderness, is a well-developed base for

Like an artist's palette, the Hyalite Basin offers a range of colors on its broad expanse of glacial outwashes. Indian paintbrush dominates this sea of green, which holds wildlife ranging from elk and moose to bald eagles and hawks. Located south of Bozeman beyond Hyalite Reservoir, the basin is a popular destination for hikers. MICHAEL S. SAMPLE

sojourns into Pine Creek Falls and Pine Creek Lake. The 10,960-foot Emigrant Peak rises above the valley floor, a crowning giant that can be viewed by swimmers in the tepid pool at Chico Hot Springs. A handful of other summits — Monument Peak, Elephanthead Peak, Mount McKnight, Mount Delano, and Mount Cowan — can be climbed from either side of the range. Campgrounds at East Boulder, Falls Creek, Aspen, and Chippy Park are logical places to plan forays into the Absaroka-Beartooth.

Radiating with noble charm in the southwestern corner of the national forest, the Lee Metcalf Wilderness offers a collage of lakes, 11,000-foot peaks, and wildlife. The Gallatin and Beaverhead national forests in Montana, along with the Bureau of Land Management, share management of this wilderness, which is split among four units that wrap across the aged Madison Range. The 249,000-acre Lee Metcalf is shaped by rock tempered 2.5 billion years ago. The Gallatin Petrified Forest, north of the Monument Mountain Wilderness Unit, displays shards of more than 100 tree and shrub species preserved in stone.

The Taylor-Hilgard Unit of the Lee Metcalf Wilderness figures prominently in the backcountry itineraries of many recreationists. The weathered slopes of the Madison Range, revealing ribs of granite, contain rock formations that are among the oldest in the Greater Yellowstone area.
MICHAEL S. SAMPLE

Nature sculpts its priceless beauty in all seasons on the Gallatin National Forest. The summit of Henderson Mountain — at 10,340 feet — yields views of snowdunes and cornices as sundown nears.
ROBERT H. SMITH

This wilderness borders the Cabin Creek Recreation and Wildlife Management Area, abutting the shores of Hebgen Lake. Grizzlies, black bear, moose, elk, deer, and bald eagles are common in the Cabin Creek drainage, making it one of the top wildlife viewing areas in the entire ecosystem.

Perhaps the aesthetic trophies of the wilderness are the pointed spires of the Spanish Peaks, an ensemble of summits that offer panoramic views of the Montana-Idaho border. Cowboys Heaven, located outside the northern cusp of the wilderness, contains a breathtaking mixture of sheer granite walls and arid scrub brush.

The Gallatin is more than just a pretty setting, however. It's also a working national forest, where natural resources drive the pulse of local communities. Since 1946, one billion board feet of timber has been harvested to supply wood for thousands of homes and commercial uses nationwide. Almost 305,000 acres of the national forest are considered suitable for logging. The Gallatin currently emphasizes harvesting trees that have been killed by fire or the mountain pine beetle and mature trees that have passed their peak growth period.

Mining for precious metals has also played an important role here. Artifacts from early mining days are scattered across the Gallatin, testaments to the boom towns that blossomed almost overnight and then evaporated into ghost towns when gold and silver deposits grew scarce. Places such as Yellowstone City, Independence, Trail Creek, and Cinnabar have all but disappeared from the map.

The same geologic influences that built the region's mountains left behind enormous banks of minerals. Embedded within the Beartooth Mountains is a gigantic fold of platinum and palladium stretching for nearly twenty-eight miles. Known as the Stillwater Complex, the deposit reaches across the Gallatin and adjacent Custer National Forest and is one of only three known platinum and palladium deposits in the world. Private companies exploring the deposits hope to reach the rare minerals by drilling a horizontal, underground shaft 19,000 feet from the East Boulder drainage into the heart of the Beartooths.

The Gallatin also has registered 1,600 gold and silver claims, the most of any national forest in the Greater Yellowstone area. Gold fever has returned to the historic mining town of Cooke City, at the northeast entrance to Yellowstone National Park, as modern mining techniques have made it easier and more profitable to extract ore. Originally dubbed "Shoofly" in

1869, the town was later named for Northern Pacific Railroad financier Jay Cooke, Jr. The substantial veins of gold buried in the alpine hillsides outside of Cooke City have attracted thousands of miners for more than a century. Current exploration efforts center around Daisy and Lulu passes.

The Gallatin high country also holds herds of grazing cattle. Although the Montana cowboy has been romanticized in literature and film, the Gallatin remains a source of historical authenticity for the notion of range riders and cattle drives. In 1866, Nelson Story drove the first herd of Texas cattle into Montana, giving birth to the livestock industry in the state. During the early part of this century, tens of thousands of cattle, sheep, and horses grazed what is now the national forest, creating erosion problems and occasional run-ins with grizzly bears. Grazing remains an integral part of the national forest heritage, but livestock numbers are a fraction of what they once were.

Of all the wild denizens in Greater Yellowstone, the grizzly perhaps draws the most mixed reactions. The massive, powerful bears are viewed with both fear and awe. Adult grizzlies stand 3.5 to 4.5 feet tall and weigh roughly 600 pounds. About 1,000 of the large, cinnamon-colored bruins survive in the lower forty-eight states — 200 of them in and around Yellowstone National Park. The Gallatin ranks second only to the Bridger-Teton National Forest in providing exceptional grizzly habitat outside of Yellowstone. Grizzlies are found across one-third of the national forest, and bear experts say their range is growing.

Hugging Yellowstone on two sides, the Gallatin provides critical habitat for many rare plants, migratory animals, and federally protected wildlife such as the grizzly. Its rangeland is considered one of the most important areas for wildlife in the West, and

A snow camper pitches a tent near Daisy Pass in the Gallatin, within view of the triangular point of Crown Butte. This area north of Cooke City is a popular winter recreation center for cross-country skiers and snowmobilers. GEORGE WUERTHNER

more than 300 species of mammals, birds, and fish have been identified here. With the exception of the non-native caribou and the once-present gray wolf, the Gallatin is home to nearly every large mammal species in the lower forty-eight states. In Greater Yellowstone, the Gallatin also contains the most combined winter and summer range for moose, bighorn sheep, and mountain goats.

High among the sharp-toothed peaks that dominate the Gallatin's horizon, reclusive mountain lions, bighorn sheep, and Rocky Mountain goats enjoy security and solitude. Half of all the mountain goats in the region live in the Madison and Absaroka ranges. Each autumn, as snow piles up in the Yellowstone Park high country, herds of elk, deer, and antelope move across the national park border into the national forest. Wildlife watchers welcome the convergence on the wind-blown floor of Paradise Valley along the Yellowstone River and outside of West Yellowstone, Montana.

But private development in these areas has reduced the amount of winter range available to wildlife. Many choice river bottoms and flat meadows have been converted into ranches and subdivisions. In the wake of diminishing habitat, an increased emphasis has been placed on the role of national forests in protecting winter range. The Gallatin is a leader in securing habitat for big game animals and has actively sought cooperative agreements with private landowners to allow elk,

King of the Gallatin's high country, the shy mountain goat reigns over craggy peaks that few hikers dare to traverse. Some mountain goats have descended from animals transplanted to the national forest for hunting purposes during the 1950s. MICHAEL S. SAMPLE

A rainbow spans the Gallatin's Paradise Valley, an area reaching from the outskirts of Livingston to the northern edge of Yellowstone National Park. The Yellowstone River cuts through this valley, which lies between the Gallatin and Absaroka mountain ranges. TOM MURPHY

AN EARTHSHAKING EVENT

Each year, thousands of minute temblors shake the Greater Yellowstone region, which lies across several geologic faults that come together around Yellowstone National Park. Few of these earthquakes are powerful enough to be felt on the surface. However, seismologists know these faults hold tremendous potential for a catastrophic quake.

Just such an event occurred August 17, 1959, when an earthquake measuring 7.1 on the Richter scale jolted the mountains of southeastern Montana at twenty-three minutes before midnight.

Within seconds, mammoth blocks of earthen crust buckled, spurring landslides and chaos on the southern end of the Gallatin National Forest. Mashed into rubble, a portion of U.S. Highway 287 slid into Hebgen Lake. At Rock Creek campground, a mountain face gave way and slid into the valley, killing twenty-eight people. And a new lake — subsequently named Quake Lake — formed when layers of fallen metamorphic rock plugged the Madison River.

Geologists said at the time that enough earth rumbled into the Madison Canyon and across the Madison River to fill the Rose Bowl stadium ten times over. The quake reverberated through eight states, and one physicist estimated that its power equaled 2,500 atomic bombs.

The Forest Service has set aside approximately 37,800 acres — including earthquake-related hiking trails and a visitor center — as a testament to this historic event. Most of the major earthquake features can be seen from U.S. Highway 287 and along U.S. Highway 191. Evidence of the quake also can be seen along the hiking trails leading to Cabin Creek, Kirkwood Creek, and Red Canyon. The Beaver Creek and Cabin campgrounds are located inside the earthquake area, and campsites exist along Hebgen Lake as well.

Bare rock in the Madison Canyon tells a tale of nature. This section is the earthquake scarp, where two pieces of the mountain slid past each other. MICHAEL S. SAMPLE

deer, and antelope to graze on ranchlands during the harsh winter months. As a result, big game herds have remained healthy, and the Gallatin has become renowned for its excellent hunting. Some 80,000 hunter days are recorded by elk hunters alone.

The Gallatin is even better known, however, for its trout fishing. Historians have referred to the national forest as "the land between the rivers." With 1,052 miles of riffled stream channels and 18,800 acres of lakes, the Gallatin offers one of the most prolific fisheries in North America. More than 125 miles of rivers are regarded as Class One streams, a rating given to waterways with exceptional fish habitat.

For visitors skilled in the art of rod and reel, the names Gallatin, Madison, and Yellowstone conjure up dreams of big trout and untamed waters. All three of those extraordinary rivers skip across the national forest, offering cutthroat trout populations that exceed 1,000 fish per mile in some stretches. The rivers also harbor rainbow, brook, golden, brown, and lake trout, as well as arctic grayling and mountain whitefish.

The Madison River, accessible by U.S. highways 87 and 287, swings west out of Yellowstone National

Few visitors to the Gallatin are likely to spot a mountain lion, although the national forest lies in the midst of mountain lion country. The large carnivores sometimes leave signs of their presence behind on the trail, through footprints, scat, or the remnants of small birds or mammals that have been their prey. JESS LEE

A clear alpine lake reflects the clouds in Montana's big sky. The lake, one of a chain known as Skytop Lakes, lies in the high, rocky terrain of the Absaroka-Beartooth Wilderness. MICHAEL S. SAMPLE

Monkshood, a blazing fury of violet, is often found near the banks of streams. Although monskhood is common in the Gallatin and throughout the Pacific Northwest, the Gallatin contains several dozen species considered rare or federally protected. PAT O'HARA

Park toward Hebgen Lake and then makes a stutter step northward toward the flyfishing mecca of Ennis, Montana. The Gallatin River, crashing beneath the Madison and Gallatin mountains, also leaves Yellowstone Park and follows a moody canyon floor composed primarily of tertiary volcanic rock. U.S. Highway 191 runs parallel to the river as it meanders north. Fifty miles to the east, across the Gallatin Range, the Yellowstone River snakes out of the national park near Gardiner and on through Paradise Valley and Livingston.

The rivers are renowned for their world-class fishing, drawing thousands of anglers to their banks each year. By the mid-1990s, the Gallatin is expected to become the number one national forest for sport fishing in the Greater Yellowstone area, with angler days surpassing 220,000. To preserve the outstanding fishing resource, the Montana Department of Fish, Wildlife and Parks has placed special regulations on the rivers, including slot limits, catch and release requirements, and bans on bait fishing.

These three rivers also offer opportunities for whitewater rafting and scenic floats where chances of spotting eagles and osprey are high.

Sprinkled across the national forest are reminders of another era in the Gallatin's history, when the concept of setting aside public lands was still new. The Main

Boulder Ranger Station is one such jewel. Located on the Big Timber Ranger District, the cozy 14 x 14-foot cabin was built in 1905, as headquarters for the Absaroka District of the 300,000-acre Yellowstone Timberland Reserve. When the reserve was later consolidated into the national forest system, the cabin served rangers in the Absaroka National Forest and, finally, the Gallatin. Built of lodgepole pine and chinked with soil, the building is one of the oldest government structures in the Gallatin backcountry.

Visitors to the Gallatin can generally find recreation within twenty minutes of major population centers. From Bozeman, where the national forest headquarters are located, the Bridger Range and Hyalite Canyon area fan out into a half moon around the city. The Hyalite region, to the south of Bozeman, offers cool, alpine forests and bubbling streams. During the spring, summer, and autumn, backpackers and mountain bikers gravitate to trails that weave along a half dozen drainages. In winter, cross-country and telemark skiers revel in tranquility. Snowmobilers also make use of unplowed roads and trails in the area.

At one end of Hyalite Canyon lies the 200-acre Hyalite Reservoir, a man-made lake built to provide the city of Bozeman and area ranchers with a fresh, stable supply of water. The shimmering surface draws

Campers and their llamas stop along the quiet shores of Campfire Lake. Many recreationists have begun to use llamas to pack supplies along on backcountry trips, because they have less of an effect on the land than horses. ROB OUTLAW

A Yellowstone cutthroat trout can be spied through the clear water that characterizes many of the rivers and streams on the Gallatin. The fish has been designated a sensitive species, because of its limited distribution on the national forest. As such, it receives special attention to prevent it from becoming a threatened or endangered species. MICHAEL S. SAMPLE

The Slough Creek Cabin, built by the Forest Service in the early part of the twentieth century, stands in a flat expanse of land known as Frenchy's Meadow just north of Yellowstone National Park. The cabin lies within the Absaroka-Beartooth Wilderness and is still used by trail crews, inspectors, wildlife researchers, and other Forest Service personnel. TOM NELSON

wind surfers and swimmers hardy enough to withstand frosty dips. Stocked generously with trout, the reservoir offers anglers good action among bends away from the developed beachfronts. The national forest, in conjunction with the Lions Club and others, has taken great care in making Hyalite Canyon accessible to handicapped visitors. The area contains paved hiking paths and fishing piers. Stretching from the reservoir like spokes on a bicycle are mountainous spines that become increasingly rugged, providing tempting terrain for climbers.

Numerous effervescent waterfalls tumble through the Hyalites, including Alpine Falls, Arch Falls, and Champagne Falls. Moose, elk, and deer regularly forage in the nearby meadows that, by mid-July, blaze with lupine and columbine. Alert visitors may also see a grizzly or mountain lion if they are lucky. Mystic Lake, located off a trail leading from Bear Canyon Road, delights many who may also want to survey the Gallatin Valley from 8,331-foot Mount Ellis. Those with a yen for primitive camping conditions can ven-

ture into the Hyalite-Porcupine-Buffalo Horn roadless area that is surrounded by a checkerboard pattern of lands in private and public ownership. The South Cottonwood area — heralded in Robert M. Pirsig's popular novel, *Zen and the Art of Motorcycle Maintenance* — also has a loyal following.

To the north of Bozeman just outside of Greater Yellowstone are the Bridgers, a rounded line of mountains whose western slope opens onto the scenic Gallatin Valley and whose east face contains Bridger Bowl Ski Area. Montana Highway 86 running at the foot of Bridger Bowl is one of the most pastoral drives in the Bozeman area. Each year, thousands of hikers traverse the Bridger Mountain "ridge trail," which is accessible from either side of the range.

Travelers to Montana and other Western states will discover the alphabet soup of acronyms that cling to mountains on the outskirts of towns. The Gallatin offers the famed "M," signifying the presence of Montana State University in Bozeman. A heavily used trail leads to the "M" from the Bridger Canyon Road northeast of town.

Soaring inside the Bridgers about twenty miles north of Bozeman is the cone-topped crest of 9,670-foot Sacagawea Peak, named for the Indian woman who guided Lewis and Clark on their journey. Climbers can head up Sacagawea Peak from a trail at the Fairy Lake Campground.

Continuing north along the Bridger Range, the isolated pinnacles of the Crazy Mountains can be seen in the azure sky. The southern Crazies, whose lofty summits rise beyond the northern tier of the Greater Yellowstone area, are considered a spiritual sanctuary in the Gallatin by Native Americans. Eight different tribes shared the national forest lands in and around the Crazies for centuries. Archaeologists digging for fire rings have dated artifacts from nomadic, prehistoric tribes to 12,000 years ago.

The Gallatin offers adventure to visitors in every season of the year. Winter here merely means a change of color from green to white in the landscape. The national forest is popular with snowmobilers, who can take advantage of more than 425 miles of marked trails. National forest trails leading to West Yellowstone, the self-proclaimed "snowmobile capital of the world," link with trail systems in Yellowstone Park and the Targhee National Forest. The steeper terrain is enjoyed by cross-country, telemark, and downhill skiers.

Big Sky, a world-class destination resort located fifty miles south of Bozeman, has more than fifty-five miles of vertical skiing over two mountains and forty miles of groomed cross-country trails on nearby Lone Mountain Ranch. Big Sky itself is privately owned, but the national forest manages the surrounding area. Bridger Bowl, sixteen miles northeast of Bozeman, is also popular with skiers. It boasts short lift lines and more than 2,000 vertical feet of runs.

Cross-country and telemark skiers can find solitude in a number of areas of the Gallatin, particularly around Bozeman and Livingston.

Visitors to this national forest are affected by its spiritual beauty, felt thousands of years ago by the Indians who once lived here. Those who travel here now soon discover that the land between the rivers and within these mountainous horizons has a captivating presence. ■

A Steller's jay, pausing here on a tree branch, is easy to identify. It's the only jay west of the Rocky Mountains to sport a crest. The Steller's jay also can be heard mimicking other birds, such as loons and hawks.
MICHAEL S. SAMPLE

GALLATIN
NATIONAL FOREST DIRECTORY
GREATER YELLOWSTONE AREA

POINTS OF INTEREST

HYALITE RESERVOIR south of Bozeman features fishing, camping, and boating, as well as special trails for handicapped visitors.

MADISON RIVER CANYON EARTHQUAKE AREA is located on U.S. Highway 287 between Ennis and West Yellowstone. Includes a special visitor center with information on the major earthquake that killed twenty-eight people and created a new lake.

GALLATIN PETRIFIED FOREST just outside the northern boundary of Yellowstone National Park contains more than 100 species of petrified trees.

WILDERNESS AREAS

ABSAROKA-BEARTOOTH About 575,000 acres on the Gallatin, running along the eastern rim of Paradise Valley.

LEE METCALF About 140,000 acres on the Gallatin, including portions of the petrified forest.

RECREATIONAL OPPORTUNITIES

HIKING AND RIDING More than 2,000 miles of trails for hiking and horseback riding. Mountain biking is permitted on many trails and dirt roads in non-wilderness sections, but check with local ranger districts for any restrictions.

CAMPING Thirty-seven campgrounds across the forest.

RECREATIONAL CABINS Fourteen cabins available for rent during various times of the year. Contact local ranger districts for information and reservations.

SCENIC DRIVES The Beartooth National Forest Scenic Byway (U.S. Highway 212) begins just outside the border of the Gallatin at Cooke City and ascends Beartooth Pass on the way to Red Lodge. U.S. Highway 89 runs through the heart of the picturesque Paradise Valley, between Livingston and the north entrance of Yellowstone National Park. The highway is flanked by the Absaroka and Gallatin mountains. U.S. Highway 191 south from Bozeman to West Yellowstone passes through the majestic Gallatin Canyon, which offers good wildlife viewing, and meanders beside the Yellowstone River.

KAYAKING AND RAFTING The Gallatin, Madison, and Yellowstone rivers all offer opportunities for whitewater and scenic floats. The Gallatin south of Bozeman also is known for its moderately difficult kayaking.

HUNTING Elk, deer, antelope, moose, mountain goats, bighorn sheep, and upland game birds. A license is required from the Montana Department of Fish, Wildlife and Parks.

FISHING The famed Gallatin, Madison, and Yellowstone rivers all flow through the national forest and are renowned for their trout fisheries. Opportunities also available on secondary streams and 18,800 acres of lakes, including Hyalite Reservoir. Montana state licenses required. Check on special regulations pertaining to catch and release or slot limits.

ALPINE SKIING Bridger Bowl (five chairlifts and one rope tow), northeast of Bozeman, and Big Sky Resort (two gondolas, five chairlifts, and one rope tow), along U.S. Highway 191 south of Bozeman. Big Sky is on private property but is surrounded by national forest lands.

CROSS-COUNTRY SKIING Numerous possibilities along the 2,000 miles of summer trail, which are ungroomed in the winter. Developed areas around Big Sky, Bridger Bowl, and West Yellowstone. Backcountry and telemark skiing throughout the national forest. Check with local ranger districts for information on snow and avalanche conditions.

SNOWMOBILING More than 200 miles of groomed trails feeding into trail systems on the Targhee National Forest and Yellowstone National Park. The Gallatin provides ready access to West Yellowstone, which bills itself as the snowmobile capital of the world. The Two Top National Recreation Trail crosses both the Targhee and Gallatin national forests before climbing to the summit of Two Top Mountain.

OFF-ROAD VEHICLES Trail bikes are allowed on several trails and secondary dirt roads, but check with local ranger districts for more details.

ADMINISTRATIVE OFFICES

FOREST HEADQUARTERS Federal Building, Box 130, Bozeman, MT 59771, (406) 587-6701

BIG TIMBER RANGER DISTRICT P.O. Box A, Big Timber, MT 59011, (406) 932-5155

LIVINGSTON RANGER DISTRICT Route 62, Box 3197, Livingston, MT 59047, (406) 222-1892

GARDINER RANGER DISTRICT P.O. Box 5, Gardiner, MT 59030, (406) 848-7375

BOZEMAN RANGER DISTRICT 601 Nikles Avenue, Box C, Bozeman, MT 59715, (406) 587-6920

HEBGEN LAKE RANGER DISTRICT P.O. Box 520, West Yellowstone, MT 59758, (406) 646-7369

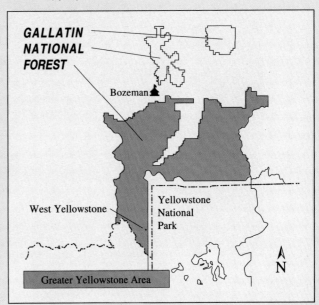

The buckling folds of Hellroaring Plateau in the Custer National Forest have trapped water left behind by retreating glaciers, creating hundreds of clear, cold, mountain lakes. MICHAEL S. SAMPLE

Custer

Inspiration from on high

The Custer National Forest in southcentral Montana is regarded as the crown jewel of high-elevation forest lands in the northern Rockies. A paradise for outdoor recreation, it sits atop one of the largest natural ecosystems in the lower forty-eight states. The Custer also boasts the tallest summit in Montana and offers the ultimate alpine drive in the nation.

As one of seven national forests in the Greater Yellowstone area, the Custer has gained international acclaim for its wonderful contradictions. Its boundaries extend more than 600 miles across three states, yet its land mass totals less than 2.5 million acres. Arresting mountain summits rocketing 12,000 feet above sea level gird the western corner of the national forest, while the eastern tier lies within ancient grasslands on the open prairie. The Custer also contains one of the wealthiest pockets of minerals in the world, as well as a pristine wilderness area without rival in the West.

Only 520,000 acres of the Custer's Beartooth Ranger District lie within the Greater Yellowstone region. Cushioned between the Gallatin National Forest in Montana and the Shoshone National Forest in Wyoming, this region nourishes a tundra environment unlike any other area in Greater Yellowstone. Grizzly bears, bald eagles, and sure-footed bighorn sheep wander here among a

The dramatic and enchanting landscape of the Absaroka-Beartooth Wilderness draws thousands of recreationists each year. Custer National Forest officials have undertaken educational activities to promote low-impact use of the area, to ensure it remains unspoiled despite its high use. LINDA CAUBLE

constellation of active glaciers, feathered cirques, and broad plateaus. Enduring the long winters and blossoming during the abbreviated growing season are dozens of rare plants known to inhabit Alaska 2,000 miles to the north.

In 1978, Congress recognized the incomparable beauty of the Custer by setting aside a substantial portion of the Beartooth Range as federal wilderness. The upper headwaters of the Stillwater River and several peaks were incorporated into the Absaroka-Beartooth Wilderness. Today more than 60 percent, or 340,000 acres, of the Greater Yellowstone portion of the Custer is classified as wilderness — the highest wilderness percentage of any national forest in Greater Yellowstone.

The Custer shares management of the 930,000-acre Absaroka-Beartooth with the Gallatin and Shoshone national forests. But the Custer contains the highest reaches of this land of skyscraping pinnacles and river-filled valley bottoms. Twenty-five peaks soar above 12,000 feet, with 12,799-foot Granite Peak towering above them all to claim the title of the tallest point in Montana. Adventurers first reached the mountain's summit in 1923. Climbers today continue to mount drives to the top, and hikers scramble across the lower, craggy pitches. Like most of the other spires in the range, Granite Peak is capped with snow for much of the year. From this mountain and any of the surrounding pinnacles, the panoramic profiles of the region's other mountain ranges are visible, including the Gallatins, Madisons, and even, on a clear day, the Tetons in Jackson Hole, Wyoming.

In the southeastern corner of the wilderness rises 12,204-foot Mount Rearguard. Nestled among a string of lakes, this peak requires a strenuous hike but rewards the climber or backpacker with a breathtaking view of Montana and Wyoming.

The Custer contains 180 miles of hiking trail that weave through even the loneliest reaches of the wilderness. Practically every drainage on the national forest contains campsites and trails that lead into the heart of the Absaroka-Beartooth. Despite its remote location, the wilderness draws numerous visitors. Not long ago, forest managers worried about overuse on many wilderness trails. Backpackers hearing of the spectacular surroundings poured into the wilderness, causing problems with litter and resource damage. But a special program aimed at minimizing visitor impact has produced lasting dividends, educating thousands of backcountry users about the value of keeping a clean camp and treading lightly on the land.

While maintained trails are strongly recommended for use, visitors can still see a skein of legendary routes used earlier in the region's history. The notorious Van Dyke Trail — named for miner, hunter, and explorer E.E. Van Dyke — was blazed in 1882 between Cooke City and Red Lodge. Traces of that overland route can be seen from the Beartooth Highway, a National Forest Scenic Byway. The Sheridan Trail, following the Line Creek Plateau toward Mount Maurice and descending to the bench east of Rock Creek, follows the footsteps of General Philip H. Sheridan, who was sent to the West in 1867 to lead the campaign against the Indians.

Clear and sparkling with an azure radiance typical of the Custer, hundreds of seasonal streams gather swiftness from melting snow, showering the steep

A butterfly touches down on a fireweed, above, one of the many wildflower species found on the Custer National Forest. MICHAEL S. SAMPLE

A rock climber, left, clings to the sheer face of Granite Peak, the tallest mountain in Montana. Each year, scores of climbers attempt to reach its summit. TOM FERRIS

hillsides with life-giving moisture. Wildflowers erupt as soon as the upper elevations are clear of snow in mid-July, and these high plains are home to abundant wildlife during the short summer season.

The Custer holds more than 120 species of birds and forty-five species of mammals, including the region's most powerful predator, the grizzly bear. Reclusive in their habits, grizzlies are drawn to the Custer's isolated hamlets and fish-filled streams during much of the summer. These areas on the southwestern edge of the national forest provide essential grizzly habitat. They also hold mountain goats, elk, and bighorn sheep that

pick their way nimbly across crumbling ledges.

Periodically, the watersheds draw federally protected bald eagles and peregrine falcons. The wide-winged raptors are most common along the Stillwater River, perhaps the most underrated fishing stream in the region. The national forest registers a mere 45,000 angler days, leaving five species — cutthroat, golden, brown, rainbow, and brook trout — to thrive with little pressure from anglers.

West Rosebud and Emerald lakes, which each measure about forty acres, are major fisheries in the area around West Rosebud Canyon. The Mystic Lake Res-

Snow tracks, above, tell the story of nature. A hawk successfully divebombed a rodent and flew away with the snack. Biologists say the struggle to survive a winter on the Custer can be perilous without proper protection — especially if you're a mouse.
TOM MURPHY

Brrrrrr. The ice-rimmed surface of Black Canyon Lake, left, is typical of several hundred mountain lakes that exist on the Custer National Forest above 9,500 feet. Although many are too cold and sterile to support fish populations, deep lakes such as this one teem with trout and reward anglers willing to make the trip. MICHAEL S. SAMPLE

RIDING AT THE TOP OF THE WORLD

The Beartooth Highway between the Montana towns of Cooke City and Red Lodge has been touted as the most scenic highway in all of America. And the description only modestly explains how spectacular the route really is. This stretch of U.S. Highway 212 has rightly earned its designation as a National Forest Scenic Byway.

Crossing the Gallatin, Shoshone, and Custer national forests, the road climbs over 8,000-foot Colter Pass and then builds dramatically for the stunning ascent of 10,936-foot Beartooth Pass. The winding asphalt road takes visitors within reach of the famed Clarks Fork of the Yellowstone River, the Glacier Lake Reservoir, and the Red Lodge Mountain Ski Area.

Because of deep snows and avalanche-prone slopes during the winter, the Beartooth byway closes between late October and the end of May. But when summer arrives, it offers the most popular drive in Greater Yellowstone outside of Yellowstone National Park.

In 1878, Chief Joseph of the Nez Perce passed through this region during his flight from the U.S. Cavalry. An informational rest stop has been set up along U.S. 212 for those who want to learn more about Chief Joseph's saga. Farther east in Wyoming, the highway meets the Chief Joseph Scenic Highway (Wyoming Highway 296) that runs parallel to the canyon country in the Clarks Fork River, where the Nez Perce chief brought his tribe to elude the cavalry.

Visitors might also consider a stop at the "Top Of The World" store near Island Lake. The store is open for business when the Beartooth Highway is open to traffic.

The Beartooth Highway snakes along the tops of mountains and crosses through three national forests, earning its designation as a National Forest Scenic Byway and offering travelers an unforgettable drive. CHRIS CAUBLE

ervoir just outside the wilderness was formed by a man-made dam on West Rosebud Creek.

The Custer has become a year-round recreational haven. Alpine and telemark skiers from around the country converge upon the Red Lodge Mountain Ski Area off U.S. Highway 212 to enjoy deep powder. Backcountry and nordic skiers have a wide choice of terrain, but are advised to check with the Beartooth Ranger District in Red Lodge for information about avalanche danger. Snowmobiling opportunities are limited by the steep terrain and prevalence of wilderness, although part of U.S. Highway 212 is open outside of Cooke City and Red Lodge. Winter, generally, is a sleepy time on the national forest when visitors can relax and enjoy a slower pace.

While the Custer is known for its non-motorized wilderness opportunities, it's also custom-made for visitors touring the national forest by car. Serving as the main forest artery, the Beartooth Highway (U.S. 212) between Cooke City and Red Lodge is hailed as the most picturesque highway in America. The winding asphalt road ascends the 10,936-foot Beartooth Pass and acts as a gateway to Yellowstone National Park. Another 120 miles of roadway, most of them dirt, skirt the wilderness and provide visitors with a natural starting point into the backcountry.

Throughout the unroaded frontier are remnants of the Ice Age snowfields that carved mountain settings

The Beartooth Mountains are transformed into a winter paradise for telemark and cross-country skiers who like to practice their technique on trackless slopes. The steep slopes of the Beartooths, which extend from the Absoraka Range, are prone to avalanches. Ski mountaineering is allowed on the Custer, but the Forest Service encourages visitors to know the terrain and check in with rangers before heading into the backcountry.
FRANK S. BALTHIS

often compared to the Swiss Alps. Active glaciers still hang above nearly three dozen lakes, some of which contain fish and others that are too barren and cold to support life. In 1899, the U.S. Geological Survey first reported the existence of an immense ice island called Grasshopper Glacier. The names given to that and "Hopper Glacier" stem from the discovery of locusts frozen in ice fields perhaps thousands of years earlier. Some Beartooth snowfields also have taken on a red hue, from decomposing bacteria trapped in the melting snow. When reflected against sunlight, the organisms bestow a tinted glow upon the the sheen of white. Flanking Grasshopper Glacier and shouldering a series of crescent-shaped precipices, 12,377-foot Beartooth Mountain sports a namesake shield of ice in Beartooth Glacier. This world of ice differs markedly from the southeastern corner of the Beartooth Ranger District.

The land here is marked by a Spartan elegance, manifested by the rocky expanse of Line Creek Plateau. Its spacious meadows, accentuated by lichen-covered boulders and mossy glens, contrast sharply with the Custer's 109,000 acres of coniferous woods. Both the Line Creek and neighboring Hellroaring plateaus exude tranquility. Road switchbacks leading to the crest of Hellroaring were built during World War II, when the federal government was seeking chromium ore for military needs.

This region also holds potential reserves of oil and natural gas, arousing concerns among people who want to preserve the untrammeled conditions of such places as Line Creek. The search for fossil fuels is not new to the region. Montana's first oil well was drilled in 1890 along the Custer's Butcher Creek. Today, 96,000 acres of the national forest are under lease for

Many of the peaks in the Beartooths cradle the glacial remains of the Ice Age. Grasshopper Glacier in the background is so named because scientists have discovered the remains of grasshoppers deposited in the ice thousands of years ago. BARBARA AND MICHAEL PFLAUM

A grizzly cub, above, looks toward its mother. Habitat protection in the Custer and other national forests is critical to the survival of the grizzly bear, a threatened species. ALAN AND SANDY CAREY

The East Rosebud area of the Custer, left, is considered the outer periphery of the Greater Yellowstone region. Mountains meet prairie, creating some of the finest backpacking terrain in southeastern Montana. MICHAEL S. SAMPLE

oil and gas exploration. Because Line Creek straddles the Beartooth Highway, all development proposals have come under scrutiny. Forest managers can set out stringent requirements to reduce environmental impacts and protect the region's scenic grandeur.

Steep slopes and a harsh climate have limited logging on the national forest, in contrast to most others in Greater Yellowstone. Fewer than 33,000 acres are considered suitable for logging, and just 69,000 acres are open to cattle grazing — the lowest totals of any national forest around Yellowstone Park.

The Custer's resource wealth is manifested, instead, deep beneath the surface of the ground, hidden among rock that is more than 2.8 billion years old.

Potent geological forces tempered layers of meta-morphic rock over the ages, leaving behind a potential fortune in rare minerals. Stretching for twenty-eight miles, the Stillwater Complex contains a large bed of chromium ore and one of only three known platinum and palladium deposits in the world. The complex reaches across the Custer into the adjacent Gallatin National Forest and has spurred a mining boom in several local communities. Development of a platinum and palladium mine near Nye, Montana, has created hundreds of jobs, and mining companies hope to extract millions of dollars worth of ore trapped more than two miles underground. Platinum is commonly used in pollution-control devices for automobiles.

On the southwestern front of the Beartooths near Cooke City, a second gold rush has brought mining companies back to Daisy Pass and Fisher Mountain. Underground mining has occurred here for more than a century. In fact, when Chief Joseph of the Nez Perce tribe passed through the region during his historic flight from the U.S. Cavalry in 1878, the first gold rush was already under way.

The Custer is also rich in historical artifacts. Archaeologists have uncovered fire rings dating back 10,000 years. Evidence of early hunting and gathering societies is scattered across the Absaroka and Beartooth fronts at some 120 sites. Those first inhabitants probably accompanied the large game herds that moved into the area as glaciers retreated from the upper valleys. Until French fur trappers trekked across the Beartooths in the early nineteenth century, the verdant hillsides remained summer homelands for several tribes.

The national forest derives its name from Lt. Col. George Armstrong Custer. The infamous leader fell with his troops on June 25, 1876, in a battle with the Sioux and Northern Cheyenne Indians.

It's easy to see why this land has long been revered by those who have lived here. Compared to other wildlands in Greater Yellowstone, the Custer stands alone quite literally because of the vantage it offers on the world from its lofty summits. A view from inside the Custer allows visitors to contemplate new and inspiring heights. ■

At 12,612 feet, Castle Mountain stands like a granite fortress in the Custer National Forest. The mountain is one of twenty-five peaks that rise above 12,000 feet on the national forest.
MICHAEL S. SAMPLE

CUSTER
NATIONAL FOREST DIRECTORY
GREATER YELLOWSTONE AREA

POINTS OF INTEREST

BEARTOOTH MOUNTAINS contain the highest chain of peaks within the Beartooth Range, including 12,799-foot Granite Peak — the tallest point in Montana. The landscape is accented by dozens of spectacular glaciers, lakes, and the high-tundra Beartooth Plateau.

WILDERNESS AREAS

ABSAROKA-BEARTOOTH About 340,000 acres on the Custer. Contains numerous recreational opportunities and is the third most popular wilderness in the national forest system.

RECREATIONAL OPPORTUNITIES

HIKING AND RIDING Hiking and horseback riding allowed on 300 miles of trails. Dozens of trailheads lead into the wilderness. Check with the Beartooth Ranger District for special regulations regarding horse travel.

CAMPING Developed campsites in every canyon on the face of the Beartooth Range, along with dozens of primitive or semi-primitive sites in the wilderness and backcountry.

SCENIC DRIVES The Beartooth National Forest Scenic Byway (U.S. Highway 212) between Cooke City and Red Lodge is touted as the most scenic drive in America. The route passes through the Gallatin, Shoshone, and Custer national forests and climbs over 10,936-foot Beartooth Pass.

KAYAKING AND RAFTING Limited opportunities, although kayaking is allowed on the Stillwater River.

HUNTING Excellent prospects for elk and mule deer. A license from the Montana Department of Fish, Wildlife and Parks is required.

FISHING The Stillwater River, East and West Rosebud rivers, and more than two dozen lakes offer premier trout fishing. License required.

ALPINE SKIING Red Lodge Mountain Ski Area (five chairlifts and one rope tow), west of Red Lodge on Forest Road 71.

CROSS-COUNTRY SKIING Wilderness and backcountry terrain is open to telemarking and ski mountaineering, but be mindful of avalanche conditions and check first with the Beartooth Ranger District in Red Lodge.

SNOWMOBILING U.S. Highway 212, south of Red Lodge to Cooke City, is recommended for experts only.

OFF-ROAD VEHICLES Because of the large amount of wilderness, opportunities for ORVs are extremely limited. But some trails and dirt roads are open to trail bikes in non-wilderness sections.

ADMINISTRATIVE OFFICES

FOREST HEADQUARTERS 2602 First Avenue North, P.O. Box 2556, Billings, MT 59103, (406) 657-6361

BEARTOOTH RANGER DISTRICT Route 2, Box 3420, Red Lodge, MT 59068, (406) 446-2103

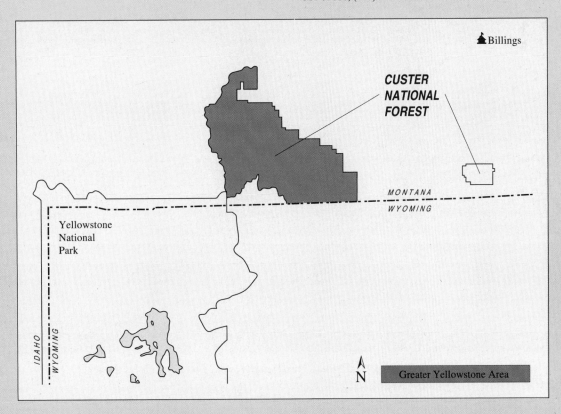

Columbine and Indian paintbrush spring unexpectedly from a crack of granite in the Targhee National Forest, transforming the sheer rock into an unexpected oasis. PAT O'HARA

Conclusion

A delicate balancing act

"*A* *lake is the landscape's most beautiful and expressive feature. It is earth's eye; looking into which the beholder measures the depth of his own nature. The fluviatile trees next to the shore are the slender eyelashes which fringe it, and the wooded hills and cliffs around are its overhanging brows.*"

— Henry David Thoreau

Like a lake in Thoreau's world, national forests offer reflections of our environment, mirroring a collective attitude toward public lands. They are places that inspire and allow each of us to benefit spiritually, physically, and sometimes even economically from the soil.

The six national forests of Greater Yellowstone represent the best intentions of people such as Theodore Roosevelt and Gifford Pinchot, who sought to establish "working preserves" in the latter half of the nineteenth century. Roosevelt and Pinchot had no delusions about why the parcels were really being set aside. Evolving from the landmark Yellowstone Timberland Reserve, those first federal forests were intended for commercial purposes, to allow for the prudent use of raw materials such as timber, minerals, grasslands, and fresh water.

Today, the same six forests, known for their natural resources, are undergoing a transformation that

The colors of every season often appear in one setting at one time in the Greater Yellowstone. Here, the snow-capped Bridger Mountains rise up out of the autumn landscape in the Gallatin National Forest in Montana. Named for explorer Jim Bridger, the mountains are in a portion of the Gallatin just outside Greater Yellowstone. MICHAEL S. SAMPLE

is changing the face of the national forest system. The Beaverhead, Bridger-Teton, Custer, Gallatin, Shoshone, and Targhee national forests together make up one of the most glorious collections of scenic beauty in the world. To perpetuate the long-term health of Greater Yellowstone's picturesque setting and incomparable wildlife, forest managers are placing broader emphasis on recreation and tourism.

While traditional uses of the national forests remain, the future of this 12 million-acre region is now based upon a management philosophy that provides for a high level of coordination with the national parks.

This approach has made developers, recreationists, and industry more responsive to the environment. The logging, mining, livestock, and oil and gas industries still contribute to the financial stability of the region. But protection of Greater Yellowstone's unique values is also factored into Forest Service decisions. As is being shown time and again in Greater Yellowstone, the two need not be mutually exclusive.

In the six national forests today, loggers are scaling down the size of their clearcuts to accommodate habitat requirements for grizzly bears and elk. Mining companies are minimizing surface disturbance to help the recovery of bald eagles. And irrigators are using less water from streams to give trumpeter swans a better chance of survival.

In America, citizens fiercely guard their favorite wooded retreats. It is a form of environmental paternalism that was first manifested in 1872 when Congress declared Yellowstone the world's first national park. Given the 5.5 million visitors traveling to Greater Yellowstone each year, the region has gained a formidable constituency.

Although the national forests are beloved by millions worldwide, the question of how best to manage them frequently pits "locals" against "outsiders" and developers against preservationists. All too often, the discussion of resource management disintegrates into a discourse on how many jobs and how much financial gain is tied to a specific use. After all, the forests were set aside to be used for a variety of purposes.

But it is difficult to place a value on a lush valley that offers refuge to elk, moose, and eagles. Or an undammed river that appears as clean today as it was when Indians took a drink from it 200 years ago. Or a marbled mountain summit that is not diminished by the haze of wood smoke or the boom of an oil drilling rig. Or a meadow blooming with wildflowers that is not covered with mineral tailings. Greater Yellowstone contains all of these unfettered vistas and more.

Ecological harmony succeeds in Greater Yellowstone because users are striking a balance. The examples are everywhere.

Following decades of severe habitat loss caused by growing development on adjacent private lands, the Forest Service and private enterprise are pooling their financial resources to acquire badly needed winter range for migratory wildlife. The federal agencies are spearheading management plans aimed at better protecting fisheries and streams. And the Forest Service and National Park Service are making decisions based on the ecosystem as a whole, rather than on jurisdictional boundaries.

The years ahead for Greater Yellowstone will be a time of reckoning. But since the Yellowstone Timberland Reserve was founded in 1890, forest management has come a long way. If Greater Yellowstone's first 100 years is any sign of what is possible in the future, the national forests here will remain global treasures for centuries to come. ∎

The jagged silhouette of the Absaroka Range, top, stands out in the afterglow of sunset on the Shoshone National Forest in Wyoming. GREG L. RYAN/SALLY A. BEYER

Water is a natural draw for wildlife. Visitors to the national forest may often spot moose wading along creek bottoms in search of leafy plants. DIANA STRATTON

HELPING YOUR FAVORITE NATIONAL FOREST

National forests are not only places of enjoyment, but also centers for learning. Each national forest has its own interpretive program, designed to help visitors learn more about its natural and cultural history and its resource management activities.

Educational opportunities and materials such as guided tours, slide shows, nature walks, exhibits, maps, and manuals are available to visitors.

Much of the material comes from non-profit interpretive associations that work closely with the national forests to provide many visitor services.

Some associations fund interpretive specialists in national forests. Others design exhibits and trail signs, while still others sell

books, trail maps, and T-shirts and use the profits to pay for projects.

Faced with budget constraints and limited personnel, the Forest Service might have to skip some of these projects without the help of the interpretive associations. If you would like to find out more about these groups, contact the following organizations:

Grand Teton Natural History Association
(Bridger-Teton and Targhee national forests)
Drawer 170-B
Moose, WY 83012
Phone: (307) 733-2880, ext. 204

Yellowstone Association for Natural Science, History, and Education
(Gallatin and Custer national

forests) P.O. Box 117
Yellowstone National Park, WY 82190
Phone: (307) 344-7381 ext. 2349

Pacific Northwest National Parks and Forests Association
(Beaverhead National Forest)
83 South King Street, Suite 212
Seattle, WA 98104
Phone: (206) 442-7958

The Shoshone National Forest is not currently a member of a regional interpretive organization, but is planning to build several of its own interpretive offices. Questions about the Shoshone and its history may be directed to the Yellowstone Association for Natural Science,

THE NATIONAL FORESTS OF AMERICA SERIES

The National Forests of America series explores the many attractions of the national forests, area-by-area. Eventually the series will cover the entire national forest system.

Each book has approximately 128 pages packed with campground and trail locations, scenic turnouts, phone numbers, addresses, and a map and directory on each national forest.

And the national forest books are illustrated with color photos from noted outdoor photographers.

Other titles in the series include *California National Forests, Montana National Forests,* and *Washington National Forests. Southern National Forests* available in April 1992.

To order the national forests books or to receive a free catalog of Falcon Press books, call 1-800-582-2665 or write to: